ECHOES
WITHIN
WALLS

YES, THEY DO TALK!

SAM RITCHIE

Dear Amanda,

Thank you for all you do!

Loads of love

Ritchie

ISBN 978-1-910027-67-7

Typesetting and cover design by Titanium Design Ltd

www.titaniumdesign.co.uk

Cover images licensed by Adobe Stock

Published by Local Legend
https://local-legend.co.uk

FOR MY PARENTS

Thank you, Mum, for teaching me always to see the bright side
and paint on a smile even when things are difficult.
Thank you, Dad, for showing me that there is only one of me
and everyone else is taken.
You both made me the person I am today and gave me the confidence
to follow my dreams. And you taught me that other people's opinions
of me is none of my business. I love and miss you both..

https://local-legend.co.uk

ACKNOWLEDGEMENTS

I would like to offer my gratitude to you, dear reader, for choosing this book and I really hope you find it informative and entertaining and that you will understand better the energies of your own property and the effects they have on you.

I am also grateful to all the angelic guides who have made my work possible and, of course, to all my clients for trusting me.

My amazing spiritual circle families have helped me to continue learning and have supported my work. I thank them all, especially Angie for challenging me, Trudy for giving me the space and quiet I needed for writing and Ginnette who helped to make this book readable!

I have had amazing teachers, notably Kyle Gray, Colette Baron-Reid and Amanda Ellie. They have not only helped me to develop my abilities and confidence, but entertained me at the same time.

Thank you, Nigel, from Local Legend for your care and support in bringing my dream of publication to reality. I know that you have gone above and beyond to help me achieve this.

Finally, and by no means least, I give heartfelt thanks and love to my wonderful family, my husband Barry and daughters Loreena and Mysty, and my Aunt Penny. You have supported and encouraged me, even though I am not always easy to live with!

https://local-legend.co.uk

ABOUT THE AUTHOR

Sam Ritchie is from the south of England. She spent more than a decade as an estate agent in the UK, always fascinated by buildings and the stories they have to tell.

But she has also always been able to see and communicate with the spirit world, which enabled her to know some of the history and character of the buildings she entered. At first, she assumed that everyone could see what she could, until she realised that it sometimes wasn't wise to talk about these things openly. Having tried unsuccessfully to bury her abilities, she finally looked for ways in which she could use her gifts to help others.

Most significantly, this took the form of clearing properties of any residual negative energies (and unwanted spiritual entities!) so that their occupants could live peacefully or sell the property more easily. She is now able to space clear remotely, using just a floor plan and address, with amazing results.

Sam is a certified Angel Guide and she also offers oracle card readings, past life regression and day retreats. She now lives in Spain with her family.

Her website is https://www.samangelguide.com/

PUBLISHER'S NOTE

By coincidence, when Sam's manuscript arrived on my desk a good friend of mine was having trouble selling his home. It was a beautiful house in a desirable location, but had been on sale for nearly a year with virtually no interest as the market was so slow at the time. This was causing my friend and his wife great anxiety due to personal circumstances.

I asked Sam to help remotely, sending her only the floor plans and address with no other information. Within a week she reported some negative energy related to the previous owners, whom she identified fully, saying she had cleared this from the property. Her description was perfectly accurate. But there were still no viewings.

Undaunted, Sam carried out a second space clearing and, within two weeks, an offer for the full asking price came out of the blue – and was accepted.

CONTENTS

INTRODUCTION

There are so many things in this world that we don't understand. I have no idea how the things I use every day such as electricity, the phone and the Internet work. Yet we get so many benefits from them and only question them if they stop working!

What about other things that we don't fully understand, such as the extraordinary power of our own minds to reach out to other states of consciousness by telepathy, remote viewing and precognition? Because science cannot yet identify the energies involved, these experiences are called 'paranormal'. Yet we have all had inexplicable things happen around us.

So it is not a big step to imagine the possibility of other, non-physical worlds and beings who could be nearby to help (and sometimes maybe hinder) us. I have come to believe that as long as we are open-minded and not fearful, everyone can have a connection with these different realms and can learn to get help and guidance in their lives. Perhaps this book will give you food for thought.

What is beyond doubt is that there are many strange energies around us, even if we cannot see, touch or feel them, and they are affecting us and the places we live in. Quite apart from the energies of nature, we project ourselves, our life force, out into the world and leave an energetic footprint on other people and places. Have you ever visited an old building or even a certain room in a modern house and immediately felt uncomfortable, somehow sensing that there has been unhappiness or even violent argument there?

This is because places have a way of storing the energies of the past, whether positive or negative. Throughout this book, I will share some of my experiences and adventures, showing you that it is indeed possible to clear negative energy from your home so that it becomes a more peaceful and happy place to live or – should you wish to move house – so that it becomes a more attractive property for buyers.

1

IF WALLS COULD TALK

When I was taken to Clearwell Castle in the Forest of Dean, UK, by my parents it was supposed to be a lovely family day out. At least, it was until we had to go up the stairs to the second floor. There was a mannequin standing on the grand staircase holding its head under its arm. This didn't help the unsettling feeling I was already getting and I refused point blank to go up. Everyone thought it was because of the dummy but no, it was the threatening spirit man standing next to him!

I stood there screaming and making a huge fuss. My parents were totally taken aback while the staff tried without success to calm me down and explain that the mannequin was not real. We never went up those stairs.

Okay, it's fair to say that I was a strange child. I spent most of my time in a world that others couldn't see, even as a small baby looking at things that were 'not there'. As a result, the world was a terrifying place for the young me. At times, people scared me and I would hide when the doorbell rang. I was never in the present moment so I would often walk into objects or not hear people talking to me. Friends and family tell me that this hasn't changed!

Strange things were always happening around me and I just

didn't see things the way others did. I was painfully shy and school was a big challenge for me. I would physically shake when I walked into a classroom because I was so terrified of what I might see. Teachers often called my Mum in as they were so concerned about me.

The second time I shocked everyone was even worse than Clearwell Castle. Aged about thirteen, I was on a school trip to Germany and the teachers, in their wisdom, decided to take us to a concentration camp just outside Berlin. For most people this would be an emotional experience, but for me it was the most overwhelmingly distressing experience of my young life. I hadn't been looking forward to this visit although I was intrigued by history. As we walked in through the gates I felt extreme sadness. Then, suddenly I could clearly see a crowd of spirit people making a beeline for me. I collapsed onto the ground screaming, my legs unable to support me. A bewildered teacher stayed with me and I never went inside.

It was mystifying to me that no-one else seemed able to see, hear and sense things that I did and it was a huge surprise to find out, around the age of twenty, that they couldn't. Everything changed overnight, though, when I simply decided that I was not going to let life scare me. I am now sure that unseen guides helped me with that, although it took many years of pushing through the fear to get to a place where I am now, where almost nothing scares me. And, as time went on, I learned how to protect my energy so that I don't get overwhelmed by the paranormal.

I have the perhaps dubious ability, then, to be aware of all kinds of energies that others cannot sense. In particular, I have come to know that the walls of our homes and the land around us echo their past. How can homes speak, you may ask? Well, have you ever walked into a room and felt uneasy or not liked the 'atmosphere' of a place however attractive it was outwardly?

In my experience, the reason for this is that every property, and even the land itself, holds a memory of what has happened there. If a property has seen sadness, pain or even violence then it retains that memory. Yes, memories of happy times are also stored but they tend to be overwhelmed by the negative. It's like a handprint in a piece of clay: the biggest hand is the print that stands out the most.

This is also why some people find graveyards 'spooky' or uncomfortable, whether or not we believe there could be spirits still hanging around, because sadness and grief have been imprinted into the land. In any case, why would a spirit want to haunt a place where their body was laid to rest? Surely it is much more likely that they would want to be in a place they have loved, near to people they loved. Naturally, there are exceptions; many believe that if someone suffered a sudden or traumatic death then they may not realise that they have passed on and will hang around in that place, being 'earthbound'.

Well, for all my oddness I was very fortunate to grow up in a family that didn't dismiss my connection to the spirit world. On the other hand, I wasn't allowed to talk about the things I saw, especially the spirit lady who lived in our house and would often sit on my bed. If I didn't pay her enough attention she would be annoyed and move things around, which scared the life out of my Mum. She refused to go to bed without leaving the landing light on. I later found out that she could also see into this hidden world.

My Dad was a complicated man who loved my Mum so much that he would do anything to protect her. It wasn't until after she passed away that he told me… wait for it… he could also see into other worlds and so could my mother! So it seems to have been a family trait. Then I learned that my Mum's grandmother used to read tealeaves, and was renowned as very accurate. I also have an aunt who is a spiritual life coach and who has been a huge support to me on my personal spiritual journey, helping me to find my true passion and purpose. She has also helped me to know that I am not a total freak!

I don't, however, refer to myself as a medium or clairvoyant and I certainly cannot call up spirits on demand. Indeed, I believe that everyone has the potential to see into the hidden realms, it's just that most people have lost the ability along the way. We are programmed from a young age not to mention these things because others will think we're weird. Yet, did you have an invisible friend as a child? Could that friend actually have been real, a spirit person or animal?

Apart from such entities, I was always fascinated by houses and I could see the energy, or aura, around some of them. It was always white and shining around the tops of buildings. There was a derelict manor house at the top of our road and I would stare at it every time I passed by, too much of a good girl to trespass. Sadly, it has long since been pulled down as have so many other beautiful buildings, gone forever. Now, one of my greatest pleasures is when a property shows itself to me in its former glory.

As well as the energies of the physical world, I have always known that there are celestial worlds and beings, including angels. I believe we all have at least one guardian angel who is with us throughout our lifetime to help, support and encourage us, and to remind us that we are loved unconditionally. For some people, this is a strange concept and one they are unable to get their heads around. But even if we don't see, hear or feel them, or even believe they are real, that's totally fine, the angels don't get offended and will still be there for us.

In fact, at first I used to be scared of connecting to angels, thinking they would be ten feet tall with unnerving powers. Having then studied the subject and had my own encounters, I have built a relationship with the angels around me and now see how silly I was. For one thing, they only show themselves in ways they know will not scare us; for me, that means I see them as small, winged silhouettes of bright white light.

They are now a big part of my life and work, gently guiding me to learn more about life and to help others to see that they are spiritual beings of energy. They also send messages through me for other people and, oddly, I hear those more clearly than the messages that are meant for me! If they are sending opportunities my way or putting ideas in my head, sometimes they have to send me the equivalent of flashing neon signs for me to take notice of them and the ideas will not go away until I have acted on them. I have now learned to trust what comes up, even if it makes no sense to me at first.

You will have heard the phrase, 'If walls could talk'. Well, guess what, they can! Think of it like this… All of us can remember a situation that was really unpleasant in our past. Unless we work hard on ourselves, we are likely to replay that situation over and over again in our heads and it will affect how we respond in some situations and towards some people. We can also remember happy events that make us smile and affect our mood. I believe that physical properties are similar in that they store the memories of past situations. In fact, it's surprising how many properties have witnessed very similar incidents, and even the same names keep cropping up.

My space clearing work offers me a unique insight into the history of properties and their past occupants. The spiritual beings I bump into along the way are always intriguing. Some want to talk, some don't realise that they're dead, some have unfinished business and some just pop in to send love to family and friends.

On the other hand, some others are malevolent and want to cause trouble. These can quickly be neutralised and moved on. They may resist but, given the army of angels and guides who work through me, they have no choice but to leave, moving 'to the light' where the soul is able to continue its development.

All these spirits offer so much by coming forward and giving great insights into the past. I am truly grateful to each of them, even the nasty ones.

I have had the privilege of space clearing a large number of properties and the histories they share and the spirits I've met along the way have been truly amazing. Buildings have revealed to me what they used to look like, many of the significant events that have taken place there, and secrets that some owners would not want to become public knowledge. In this book I shall share all this with you. Exact locations, though, will not be revealed in order to protect the privacy of both the current and past occupants, with the exception of two properties where I have been given permission to identify them.

So what is space clearing? It is a ritual used to move energy and has been performed in many different ways and in many different cultures throughout history. As described before, we all respond to energy with some places making us feel light, uplifted and happy whilst others make us feel drained, depleted and uncomfortable. Clearing the energy has a positive influence on the way we feel and on our lives moving forward.

Ancient peoples understood the power of space clearing and it was an important part of their lives. Native Americans used drums, rattles and burning herbs to change the energy, whilst the Chinese used gongs, chanting and incense. In mediaeval Europe they used salt and prayer. In the Middle East it would be common to use smouldering resins like frankincense and myrrh.

Personally, I use a mixture of the ancient traditions, always starting with sound which has the mystical ability to restore harmony. That is also why so many religions and cultures use bells or singing in their practices to move energy. Throughout Christianity, church bells have not only been used to call people to services but were also believed to ward off dark forces.

I begin by clapping my hands, from a quiet and muffled sound to being crisp, sharp and clear. Usually, I can hear the energy change immediately. (Try it now in your room and see if you can hear the difference.) I also use bells and a 'singing bowl'. These bowls date back more than three thousand years in Asia. They not only sound amazing but are believed to clear negative energy and replace it with positive.

Smoke and candles are also universal symbols of connection to spirit, burning away impurities and 'bringing in the light'. I use incense, sage and the sweet and aromatic palo santo, which is the Spanish name for bursera graveolens. Colloquially known as 'holy wood', it is a wild tree native from the Yucatán Peninsula to Peru and Venezuela. For millennia it has been known to clear negative energy, raise our vibration and enhance creativity, as well as having health benefits including reducing stress and treating pain.

However… the first thing I always do is protect my own energy.

This I do on a daily basis, sometimes multiple times. It's a great way to start the day and I recommend everyone to make it a habit too, especially if we know we have to deal with difficult people or a stressful situation later. Firstly, I call on Archangel Michael to cut any energy cords that are holding me back, using a simple prayer.

> *"Thank you, Archangel Michael, for cutting any cords*
> *that bind me to people, places, programming*
> *or any other situations that are not serving*
> *my purpose to be happy."*

Then I call on Archangel Metatron.

> *"Thank you, Archangel Metatron, for using*
> *your sacred geometry and magenta light*
> *to clear my energy, the energy of the room I am in*
> *and of the whole property."*

Sacred geometry is an ancient science of energy patterns that create and unify all things. There are a few basic geometric shapes and number patters that underlie all natural growth.

You will have noticed that when praying to the angels I always start with 'thank you'. This lets them know that we believe in them and that we trust they will do what we have asked. We should then imagine a bright white light coming down from the universe and making a bubble of protection around us, or a cascade of bright, clean water washing over us, cleansing our energy field (or aura). If you're not sure about angels, you could instead ask the universe, God, Source, Buddha, Spirit, or whatever name for a higher power feels right to you, to protect you.

> *"Thank you, universal Spirit, for showering me*
> *in your white light. Thank you for creating*
> *a bubble of protection around me*
> *so I am safe and protected. And so it is."*

I love using crystals, too, and I just can't get enough of them! In deciding which ones to choose, we should always just go for the ones we are drawn to by our intuition. There are many books and Internet sites describing crystals and which ones work best for particular situations. Whenever I do look them up, it normally turns out that the ones I've chosen are perfect for my intended use or for how I am feeling.

Before using or wearing any crystals, though, we must cleanse and charge them and there are many ways to do this. We can hold them in saltwater, as long as they aren't water soluble, or we can hold them over the smoke of incense, sage or palo santo. They can be charged in sunlight or moonlight, although strongly coloured crystals may lose some of their colour if left them for too long in bright sunlight.

My favourite, and the quickest, way to cleanse and charge crystals is the practice I do every day. It simply works by intention, always the key for any spiritual work. I hold the crystal in my hands and visualise any negative energy moving up through my hand, down my body and out through the soles of my feet, being taken down to Mother Earth and transmuted. Then I visualise the new positive energy coming up through the soles of my feet, up my body, down my arms and into the crystal I am holding. Finally I visualise the pure energy of the universe flowing down through the top of my head, into my body, along my arms and into the crystal.

I also speak to my crystals whenever I wear them and, for those I keep under my pillow, each time I change the linen and, of course, whenever I'm about to use them in my work. The words will change according to the situation and whatever I'm doing that day, just to keep me safe.

> *"Thank you, crystal, for helping me clear*
> *the energy of this property and of all those*
> *who live or enter it. And so it is. Thank you."*

When I arrive at a property I must first decide where to start, perhaps the first room I find myself entering or the most central area of the place, whatever feels right. I set up a small altar with my incense, sage, palo santo, bells, crystals and singing bowl. This will be my base while space clearing. I now call in the angels and my guides; after all, they're the ones doing the work and I am just the vehicle they use to remove any negativity. Who to call on can vary according to the situation but it's normally the archangels Michael and Metatron, then other appropriate angels and guides. For example, I often work with Lord Ganesh if there seems to be an obstacle to a property selling.

> *"Thank you, angels and guides, for revealing*
> *what I need to know about this property.*
> *Thank you for helping me clear away any*
> *negative energy present.*
> *I am only open to the highest and best influences.*
> *I am safe, I am protected."*

As described earlier, with my intention to clear any stagnant or negative energy I start to clap, work my way around all the walls, paying attention to the corners as energy often gets stuck there. I keep doing this until I can hear the change. With incense burning on my altar, using sage and palo santo, next I move the smoke around with my hand. This tends to be when I receive the most information.

Images related to the property appear in my head or sometimes voices give me details. I take my time over this to ensure that I have received everything I need to know. Sometimes this can be difficult, leaving me feeling breathless, crying, dizzy or occasionally even a little scared. However, I trust that I am protected. When things have been especially difficult, I can see a circle of angels around me showing themselves as light, almost like a Christmas angel paper chain, shining brightly and holding hands in a protective circle. It is strange and beautiful to see, and it does reassure me that I am safe in the most magical way.

Now we have to move the energy so I pick up the bells and work my way around the walls, projecting their sound with my intention, before moving on to the singing bowl. This creates harmony, the sound smoothing any energy that is disturbed and bringing beautiful peace and calm to the property.

When it's time to programme the property, I always do this with a prayer, the words depending on the reason for the space clearing. I always start by thanking the angels, guides and beings of light for their help. (Just as with affirmations, I am thanking them as though the work has already been done because that shows true intention, belief and trust.)

If there have been earthbound spirits, I give thanks for helping them move to the light. If the property is on the market, I give thanks for a quick and successful sale. If it's a business that wants to grow, I give thanks for that. These prayers are always for the highest good of all, for the best possible outcome for everyone involved and for the property to be healthy, happy and abundant.[1]

The results are often amazing.

One property had been on the market for two and a half years with very little interest. Within a week of my space clearing, an offer was accepted and the deposit was paid. The strangest thing

---

[1] You may like *Angel Prayers* by Kyle Gray (Hay House, new ed. 2018)

about this case was that the property was sold through an estate agent who hadn't even got a contract with the vendor!

There were clients who had issues with uncooperative tenants not allowing them access. Within twenty-four hours, this was resolved. Another client had a struggling business; within a few hours, he received the call he needed to get him out of trouble. Some people just want their property to feel better, others want to enhance what is already good about it: I once cleared a hotel and programmed every bed to give the best night's sleep for the guests. Some need strange noises or smells to go, others want their pets to stop barking at nothing! There can be unexpected health benefits for property owners… one lady even lost weight after years of struggling and without changing her diet.

As you will read later, there came a point when I discovered that I could do space clearing remotely, using just a floor plan and address. I redraw the plan, which helps me tune in to the property, place crystals on it and do the same as though I were in the property in person, using clapping, bells, singing bowl, sage and palo santo. The information arrives, negative energy or troublesome spirits are removed, then I write a report and wait for the results to show up. We usually don't have to wait long.

Of course, I can't guarantee that a house will sell within a week or that its owner will lose weight! But I do know for sure that a home will feel happier and more peaceful after space clearing.

If all this seems simple – surely moving earthbound spirits to the light must be more complicated? – well, the results speak for themselves. I am not particularly special, but I have found a way to tune in to earthly and spiritual energies. I am here to help clear negativity. Think of it like electricity, the phone and the Internet… we may not understand them but we can appreciate their benefits.

2
THE ESTATE AGENT

Given my fascination with houses, it's no surprise that my first professional job was as an estate agent in London, and it soon became apparent that I had a 'gift' for selling difficult properties. I had absolutely no idea at the time that I was instinctively space clearing, just by my intention and presence. And to be fair, it took me quite a long time to realise what was going on.

Even now I can clearly remember some astonishing cases. Working for a large agency chain in London, I was once sent to supervise the viewing of a garden flat. Perhaps I should have had my suspicions when I was told to go early and take a large can of air freshener with me! This property, though, was on one of the better roads in the area, a quiet residential street lined with beautiful trees. It was a Victorian purpose-built maisonette with its own front door, and the front garden had been well cared for.

As soon as I entered it was clear that this had been a much-loved home. Yes, the smell was bad but the place was welcoming and warm. Then, when I opened the bedroom door, I was hit by an overwhelming feeling of confusion and loneliness. All the furniture had been removed here, although not in the rest of the property, but as I stood in the doorway I could see how it had looked just a few short months before. By now I was used to seeing things that others couldn't but this was rather different…

A double bed was in front of me and in it was the body of an elderly and frail woman. All her personal belongings were laid out on the bedside table – there was jewellery, a book, and even a cup that the lady had been drinking from. It took a few moments to adjust to this scene in front of me before I suddenly remembered that I only had five minutes until the viewer arrived. I opened the windows.

The old lady was of course in spirit form and it became clear to me that she was unaware that she had died. That was the feeling of confusion I had been picking up; she had passed away in her sleep and had no idea that it was time to leave her beautiful home. Gathering my wits, and taking a deep breath, I gently explained to the lady that it was time for her to move on. The room then filled with the scent of lavender and her spirit was free. It was as much a surprise to me as probably it was to her that, simply by my entering the room and recognising the situation, she could finally take the next step of her soul's journey. It was a beautiful, calming and emotional experience, and I am so grateful I was able to help her.

With the spiritual problem solved, there was still the physical one – the stench of the body – so I set to work fast, opening every window and door and using the air freshener I had been armed with. As I worked, again instinctively I set the intention for the property to be a happy and comfortable home once more. The viewers bought the property.

By complete contrast, another building I was sent to had never been a happy home. In fact it has to be said that this was the only property that has ever scared me. Definitely a project for the developers, it was just off a High Street in south London, the first in a street of Victorian terraced houses. Some had been lovingly restored to their earlier magnificence but not this one.

Moreover, it was larger than the average house on the street and, being the first on the terrace, also meant it was the noisiest. This was not only because of its position, it had been split into bedsits and some of the tenants were still living there. Today it was my job to measure up the property and prepare all the details for it to go on the market.

Before I even got through the front door I was apprehensive. This was definitely not a welcoming property and I immediately felt that sense of a presence watching me even though I'd been assured that no human beings were in. My anxiety grew as I slowly made my way around the first floor, measuring and noting down the details. When I got to the cellar stairs and opened the door, the atmosphere was so dark and foreboding there was no way that I was ever going down there! I closed the door.

I checked out the basic and dirty kitchen and the bathroom, both of which seemed to have been added to the house as a casual afterthought and certainly without love. (Yes, there was a 1970s avocado bathroom suite, but dirty and cold.)

Moving up the house to the main living area, by now I was trying my best to get out as soon as possible because 'the presence' was still following and watching me. I was in such a panic that I started to make mistakes with some of the details although, thankfully, my boss later just laughed at the description and rewrote it.

Even without my psychic senses, this house was a disappointment at every level. The windows had rusty metal frames and were single-glazed. Almost none of the original Victorian splendour remained, and even the ceiling rose was a polystyrene copy. The top floor, built into the loft space, was even worse than the other floors. The stairs going up there were narrow and certainly wouldn't pass modern regulations.

Something else that defied regulations was the pair of spirits that now confronted me. The one who had been following me around waited at the foot of the stairs, as if to cut off my escape, while his mate greeted me at the top. He showed himself to me as a tall man in dark clothing with an angry, scarred face. And he definitely wasn't happy.

I am not quite sure what happened next. Without thinking, I just told him clearly and confidently (not that I felt it) to get out of my way and to leave the building. He just left. The first spirit, a little more hesitant now, was waiting at the bottom of the stairs and I told him to leave too. As if by magic, he was gone.

Knowing what I know now, that house wouldn't worry me in the slightest but back then it seemed as though this was a big test for me, one I needed to prove I could pass. The experience was something so profound that, even all these years later, I am still surprised by it. I shall never forget that day and the two spirit men who wanted me out of their house.

It was a clear sign that I should be space clearing properties but, back then, I had never heard of such a thing. My everyday estate agency life was busy and although, yes, I seemed to change the fortunes of properties by just doing my job, I had no idea that this was my calling. It would become something I absolutely love to do, discovering the back stories of properties, especially derelict ones, and bringing them to life.

After a few adventures and the arrival of my two daughters, I would then meet someone who changed everything. I had moved closer to my home town and reconnected with an old school friend who, in turn, introduced me to her friend, Liz. Both being spiritually minded, we hit it off straight away. She was going through a difficult divorce and had two young sons, one of them with special needs. We'd meet for coffee and meaningful talks and for all the kids to play together. I was helping her and she helped me, more than she could have known.

One day I casually mentioned that our house had an uncomfortable feeling about it. I knew we didn't have any earthbound spirits but I couldn't put my finger on what was wrong or what I could do to change the energy. She told me about space clearing.

This information was mind-blowing. I had discovered in

my estate agency work that I could affect the atmosphere of a property, but that was instinctive. I didn't know that it could be done more deliberately and thoroughly.

So I set off to clear our home, at first just with hands for clapping and some sage for burning. To my astonishment, as I moved from room to room, images of pain, abuse and attempted suicide immediately became clear. I did know that the last occupants had had some 'trouble', and one of the reasons for them moving was so that their son couldn't find them. But none of us truly know, do we, the extent of the emotional and psychological imprint of the previous generations?

Downstairs was filled with memories of arguments and fear. This was not pleasant but the real secrets were found on the first floor. As I clapped my way around my daughter's room, all I could see were images of a terrified little girl hiding in the built-in wardrobe; then, in a flash, she was no longer hiding but locked in it. This might all have 'residual energy' but, as sensitive as I and my daughters are, it was clearly not a good energy to be living with.

There was worse to come. As I entered the bathroom it suddenly became a room covered in blood. It was everywhere, up the walls, and the sink was awash with it. A vision of a woman lying on the floor jumped out at me. The scene was brutal and unexpected.

I knew the spare bedroom would be another challenge. The ceiling and walls had been painted black, a clear indication of its inhabitant's poor mental health. But this was extreme. Here I saw a teenage boy so full of pain, anguish and despair; it was hard to be in that energy and my heart went out to him. He had been abused in that room, beaten and then locked in. All these experiences had taken a huge toll on his mental, emotional and physical health and he had turned to drugs to try to escape his inner demons. This energy was as strong as if it was still happening in that moment.

By the time I got to the master bedroom I was becoming

fearful of what other horrors this house would reveal. Yes, there was domestic abuse and anger but, thankfully, in comparison with the other rooms upstairs it was an easier task for me. I cleared all the energies that day, making the house a home and indeed it was a happy one for us in the following years.

When I excitedly told Liz about all I had seen and cleared, she smiled and simply pointed out to me that I had a special gift; most other people who do space clearing do not see all such details and secrets. After that, I always cleared our homes and those of the friends and neighbours around me who were having a problem with a situation in their lives or property.

Much later, it became my business, as I realised that this is a big part of my mission on planet Earth this time around.

A few more years passed with the ups and downs that inevitably come with having a human life. Then the opportunity came for us to move to Spain, to give our girls a different lifestyle. We have certainly done that! There have been many adventures, and a few misadventures, along the way. Yet there is no doubt that when I have focused on some form of spiritual practice, even if that was just journaling, things have gone more smoothly.

At first, moving to Spain was not an easy thing to do. We decided that my husband Barry would go over first and rent a holiday apartment from some friends for a week or two while he searched for somewhere for us all to live. When he took me to the first house that he had rented for us, it wasn't what I was hoping for. It was literally the only place in the tiny rural village that was available and the Internet definitely wasn't up to speed.

In areas like this there were very few or no rental properties listed and it turned out harder than we had imagined to find a place to settle. That's probably why we lived in so many properties over a short period of time, keeping our ears to the ground and moving every time something came up that was better than the last.

Sometimes I wonder whether there was another reason. Was I meant to clear the energies of these properties? Was there a Bigger

Plan being played out by the universe, one that I was oblivious to? Or maybe it was because as a child I'd always wanted to be a gypsy, much to the frustration of my Dad. He did once comment wryly that I seem to have succeeded in that aim! But my moving days are behind me now and we have lived in the same house for more than a decade with no intention of moving again. After all, I have now learned to clear the energy of a property without having to live in it.

Our first Spanish home was not welcoming in any way, shape or form, and just moving in was a trial. It was a very old village house situated down a narrow alleyway between other similar properties, most of which were abandoned. The nearest road, with no parking for cars, was two hundred metres away and down a very steep slope. To move anything we had to block the road, unload our belongings and carry them by hand up the hill to the house. Even after all that, every food shopping trip was an exercise in strength and determination. Oh Barry... trust a man not to consider such practicalities!

The house itself was dark, old, in need of renovation and... weird. One bedroom had a toilet, just a toilet, in the middle of it. Very strange. When I space cleared it, all I saw was darkness, sadness and deception. No specific information came up and no spirits were lingering there. That is, apart from the one who popped in from the old printing business across the alley, complaining that all his work was being left to rot in his old home and office. I couldn't do anything to help him with that, apart from suggesting that maybe now was the time for him to move on. He must have taken my advice because he never reappeared.

The house felt better after the clearing and the work we started to do on it to make it our home. However, we were only ever meant to be passing through and sure enough there came a day when I received a call from our landlady, telling me that she needed 'to give the house back'. What? It turned out that she had paid a deposit and been given permission to move in, but had never completed on the purchase of the property so she didn't own it after all. It seems that estate agency due diligence is not what I had been used to in the UK. The real owners were actually lovely when I explained our situation, knowing that we had taken care of the house, and didn't want just to throw us out.

That whole experience sent me into a panic because, back then, I hadn't realised that everything happens for a reason.

A much more comfortable home was in a hamlet, the whole area drenched in residual energy with every building having its ghosts of poverty, incest, struggle and mental illness. It stood in the shadow of the Civil War, yet I found it not nearly as dark as several other small villages in this area of Spain. Our hamlet had got off lightly in comparison. The house itself had been renovated, which helped to move a lot of the bad energy, and it had little to reveal. It had been in the same family for years and they were successful, escaping the many hardships that their neighbours faced in the past (and still face today). Yes, there was a spirit man who visited a lot, just to check us out, but was not stuck or worrying in any way.

Due to unforeseen circumstances – I did say that things were always taking interesting and normally difficult turns until I realised what the Bigger Plan was – the job my husband had been offered fell through. We needed an income and, with very limited Spanish, we had few options. So we took over the swimming pool bar, owned by the Town Hall. Well, why not?

Now, this was teeming with activity and most of it was coming from the land the bar was built on which had been part of the church's vegetable garden. The spirit of a priest would show up regularly and my daughters would often see him too, in the playground at the back of the bar. He was taller than the average Spanish man and always showed himself to me dressed in a long black coat with a wide-rimmed black hat.

There was also a spirit man who liked having a joke with me. I never saw him but, whenever I was in the kitchen preparing food and was alone, he would call out my name. At first, thinking it was a customer, I would leave what I was doing and rush out front, to find no-one there. Then I would hear him laughing at me. He wasn't a bad chap, just wanted some acknowledgement which I always gave him. He did get weird at times, though. Once, on a really busy day, I went to get a beer from the fridge for a customer only to be confronted by a spirit hand – just the hand, no arm. It made me jump but I knew it was just our fun-loving resident spirit.

After one of our regulars, Antonio, passed away, he started coming back to visit me. A lovely man, I called him Donkey Man because he always arrived on his much-loved donkey. We'd spent a lot of time together, he helping me with my Spanish and learning a little English from me, during many funny sessions. Unfortunately, the donkey was no match for the car that killed him and, within a few short weeks, Antonio went too.

During this time, I met a local medium who was really interested in all the spirit activity in the bar. She asked if she could bring her development circle for a visit. We had a great afternoon and Barbara was able to confirm what I thought I knew. We even did a bit of interesting table tipping, where everyone in the group gently rests a finger on the table and spirits use the energy of the people to get the table to move.

After that, I tried to focus on the normal things of everyday life, like looking after a family and trying to make a bit of money. But sure enough, whenever I let spiritual activities take a back seat, things fall apart. The bar was broken into and we had to close it down. It was becoming a pattern.

Perhaps instinctively realising that, and with time on my hands, I started once again to read spiritual and self-help books. ("About time, too," I hear the angels mutter.) This led to a conversation with some friends who told me they had a problem in their home, a really nasty smell that came and went but could at times be unbearable. I offered to space clear their home and off I went, armed with incense and bell.

The issue was clear as soon as I walked around the house. There was an old, earthbound spirit man on the stairs. He didn't know he was dead and couldn't understand why these people were in his home. He wasn't bad, just confused, and the smell occurred as a result of his frustration. I explained to him that he had died and that it was okay for him to leave now so off he went, as did the smell, which has never returned.

Another friend had a townhouse with what seems to us a rather strange problem. The energy felt really heavy there because of several blocked-off rooms. Now, that's not uncommon in Spanish houses. The reason for this is that, when someone dies, the house will usually get divided between other members of the family; but if they can't agree to sell, or one person denies access to others, they simply brick the rooms up. Several years later, this house would become very important in my work.

Looking back, it may seem strange that I had not been doing spiritual work all my adult life, but there are several reasons. A significant one is that, during the whole of my childhood, like most young people I was trying to fit in. This is difficult when you are not often on the same planet as everyone else! Moreover, I was brought up to get 'a proper job', something that was acceptable to most people, and given my fascination for properties estate agency work was deemed just about acceptable.

There was the added pressure faced by many people with spiritual gifts, the feeling of not being good enough, not being worthy enough to do such work. Finally, there were downright physical constraints. However much I really wanted, later on, to be doing more space clearing, there was a very limited market because the properties would have to be within driving distance. They would also either need to have spiritually-minded owners or such a major problem that sceptical owners would swallow their reservations.

Things changed when I started studying oracle cards, doing a lot of research and beginning a business, reading cards and carrying out past life regressions sessions. During the pandemic and the time of lockdowns, especially, so many people were in real need of guidance and comfort. I did about five hundred free readings until I realised that people would indeed pay me to do what I loved.

It would still take a while, clearing the odd property that was situated close to home, before space clearing became my main focus. And I still love reading cards, holding two spiritual circles each week in my local area that keep me on my toes. I research a different topic every week and read a card for every person who attends. I also read a card for myself every single day, to keep me heading in the right direction.

Years ago, a lovely friend suggested that I should write a spiritual book. I didn't listen to her. What would I write about? In any case, I was not good enough, not worthy enough… My friend is now in spirit, and I am sure she often visits me in a form of a beautiful small bird, sitting on the railing of my roof terrace, just as she told me she would.

3

ANGELS AND GUIDES

My Mum was diagnosed with an inoperable brain tumour. It had been a struggle to get the diagnosis as her doctor at first prescribed anti-depressants, but my Dad was insistent that something else was going on I agreed. She had gone from being the life and soul of the party to hardly communicating at all. We used to speak on the phone most days, sometimes multiple times, but she suddenly stopped calling me. When I called her, it was strained and difficult. Even her mobility was suffering, so my Dad was right, this wasn't depression.

I give this painful account because I know there are many, many other families who have had to go through experiences like ours.

A plan was hatched. I would drop my girls at school, then drive to my parents' house just as Mum was leaving to visit the doctor so I had an excuse to go in with her. I just got there as she was pulling out of the driveway and off we went. That was one scary five-minute drive and it was very evident that Mum should not be driving anymore!

Sadly, this doctor was not at all helpful or even caring. She implied that my mother had a drink problem as well as depression. I asked for my Mum to be referred for a brain scan but no, it was "not necessary" and the waiting list was at least six months anyway.

The only option was to pay for a private scan. Well, Dad would have done anything for my mother – he would have sold their house if he had to – and luckily he was a successful businessman so could financially afford this. Within a week she had the scan and within days we had the results.

The sky crashed down on our close family. It was kept a secret from others, including Mum's parents, because not everyone could be trusted to respect our privacy. Yes, everyone knew Mum was ill, they could see it, but they didn't know how bad it was. Because it was an aggressive type of tumour, she had been given just six months to live – the same time it would have taken to get a NHS scan. On the other hand, now that there was a diagnosis, she could go back to the NHS for treatment.

Dad and I were to care for her at home with the help of health professionals, although in fact the only support we got was from a wonderful occupational therapist. No-one else even came to the house. I would drop my young children at school and then go over to my parents' house while my father was at work. During school holidays the girls and I would spend more time with Mum, trying to make good memories for us all. We would go to the seaside or the park, for example, but every day was becoming more difficult as Mum was declining almost hourly. I told my young girls the truth, that Nanny was very ill.

By the time medical treatment actually started she was in a really bad way, hardly able to walk or talk, and confusing answers to even the basic yes and no questions. She was being violently sick. We stopped going out altogether.

At the next hospital appointment I went along too. The doctors asked Mum questions, even though she wasn't capable of answering, but I could hardly contain myself when Dad answered on her behalf that she was "no worse, doing fine." Still, I knew he was just clinging to the hope that he might have more time with her; I also knew that if I didn't stay quiet and go along with him he would shut me out. That would be no good for any of us.

Next day, I took over some shopping they needed and helped Mum to get dressed. She had always been a classy dresser, never leaving the house without painting on her smile, but now she needed clothes that were easy to get in and out of. She must have hated the jogging trousers and sweatshirts. When I then asked if she needed anything else, it took all her might to get the word 'Yes' out. The bathroom? She shook her head and rolled her eyes. Eventually I realised that she wanted me to come back the next day. She knew it was time…

Dad convinced me that I should bring the girls even though I didn't want to, and I cried all the way home. Then I sat in the garden with Barry and the girls, trying to explain to them that Nanny was more ill now and was going to leave us. It was heartbreaking. I also told Barry that if I sensed it was necessary for him to leave, then he must take the girls and just go, no questions asked.

The next day, I knew before we even arrived that something wasn't right by the pain deep in the pit of my stomach. As we drove up, my Dad was standing there on the phone and it was he who told Barry to go. I ran upstairs to find my Mum's almost lifeless body lying on the bed. The emergency operator was telling Dad to give her CPR and he wanted me to do it.

I just couldn't. I knew that now was the time she was meant to leave us.

We sat on either side of her, holding her, and watched as her soul left her body. Then the most beautiful thing happened. A stunning white silhouette swept down and the room was filled with light. This was the first time I'd seen an angel and it felt like time stood still. It wasn't frightening or disturbing in any way, it was peaceful, loving and the most amazing thing I had ever witnessed. The light that was her soul joined with the angel, washing all the pain away from her. She was at peace.

It was a truly a blessing to be able to see my mother leave her body and I shall forever be grateful for that.

In recent months, I had been studying the Emotional Freedom Technique (EFT), a psychological acupressure method that involves tapping specific points of the body, especially helpful for managing stress and anxiety. I had hoped that it would help Mum to transition to the next world and I believe it did. But it also helped me to get through her funeral, calming me down and stopping the tears just below the surface from rushing all over my face especially when I read out the following well-known poem in honour of the strong, brave and loving woman who raised me.

Do not stand at my grave and weep,
I am not there, I do not sleep.

I am a thousand winds that blow,
I am the diamond glints on snow,
I am the sunlight on ripened grain,
I am the gentle autumn rain.

As you awake with morning's hush,
I am the swift uplifting rush
of quiet birds in circling flight.
I am the soft star that shines at night.

Do not stand at my grave and cry,
I am not there, I did not die.

This is a slightly amended version of the original poem, *Immortality*, written by Clare Harner in 1934.

From this point I was able to sense and communicate with the spiritual world more easily. Mum doesn't often come to visit me, and when she does it is normally in dreams where she is just as she was in life. She tells me she is busy having fun and visiting different places. I do feel her around me though, and when I open her jewellery box I get a whiff of her perfume. She was certainly at the hospital when my grandfather was very ill. My Gran is the one who visits me the most. She never says anything but if I have forgotten to wind the clock I inherited from her she moves the plates on my Welsh dresser!

When my Dad died, sadly I wasn't there because it was very sudden and a huge shock to everyone. He too does now visit me, although his favourite thing to do is to confuse one of our dogs. He was a joker in life and definitely hasn't lost his sense of humour in death. My aunt and I went to a Spiritualist church a few months after he passed. He was there and kept saying to the medium that "Big bad John is here." (He was 195 cm tall.)

Resolving his estate proved to be really difficult because he had still been running a very successful business. As so often happens, the worst of humanity can raise its head in such circumstances. By now I had moved to Spain but the problems meant that I had to spend a lot of time back in the UK. I stayed in the family house, comforted by knowing that both my parents were there with me and helping me not to feel lonely away from my husband and girls.

Despite the difficulties there were new opportunities for me. I had the space to develop my own spirituality and, especially importantly, I was able to develop confidence in doing spiritual work. Nursing my mother somehow also gave me a greater sense of my own worth and strength. In the UK I was able to visit several different Spiritualist churches with my aunt and my godmother, always learning and laying strong foundations for the work I do now.

Many people believe that we choose our parents before our birth and that part of 'the plan' we sign up for is to experience difficulties that allow our souls to grow. Well, my life had not been easy when I was growing up, culminating in the loss of my parents, yet I shall be eternally grateful for all the love and support they gave and continue to give me.

Since that turning point in my life, I have learned and experienced much more about the angels and spiritual guides around us, and

31

they've been more than valuable in my work.

Angels have featured in most cultures and religions throughout history, depicted as spiritual beings of light everywhere from ancient caves to modern churches. They may be called by different names and described in different ways, but most people see them as intermediaries or messengers between God, Source or Spirit, and humanity.

With halos representing holy light and wings for travelling between the higher worlds, the definition of angels is up for interpretation and we must each follow what feels true for us.

Some spiritual teachers say that a *bodhisattva*, a person or soul on the path to awakening, is an angelic being. Others refer to the *devas* as divine beings in Buddhist and Hindu religions. The Japanese call angels *kami* whilst in Judaism they are the *malakim*, messengers of God who help Him to carry out His intentions. Mormons believe that their founded Joseph Smith was visited by the angel Moroni who led him in creating the *Book of Mormon*. Angels are important in Islam, referred to as *malaika*, the messengers from Allah to the world, and it is believed that the angel Jahra 'il revealed the *Qur'an*.

Angels play a huge role in Christian faiths, with the Archangel Gabriel announcing the birth of Jesus and others protecting him in the wilderness. The *Book of Revelation* refers to the Nine Choirs of Angels hierarchical system, the roots of which go back to Zoroastrianism.

My own belief is that it is rather simpler than this, that we have the archangels who then call in other angels to help us when they are needed, bringing nothing but love with them and reminding us that we are all connected. This means, in the spiritual worlds, that angels are omnipresent so you can still work with them while I do, which is handy.

Of course, there are many differences between faiths but also, at their heart, many similarities. (How wonderful the world could be if we only recognised how alike we are.) Angels transcend religion and dogma, they do not discriminate between people, and they don't even care whether we believe in them or not!

A common belief is that angels have never lived human lives. Our loved ones who have passed on may feel like our 'guardian angels' but my understanding is that they are better thought of as spirit guides. On the other hand, I think we all do have at least one guardian angel who has been with us through every lifetime and who knows us better than we know ourselves. Perhaps we draw others to us if we are having really traumatic experiences, who may only stay with us for a period of our life or decide to continue beside us throughout our soul's journey.

Carl Sagan has said that we all come from the stars and that we have stardust in our DNA. Sometimes I like to imagine how our first meeting with an angel went: there we were, sitting on a star with another being sitting on a different star, so we get chatting and decide that one of us is going to incarnate on Earth and the other is going to be our guardian angel. Of course, it may not be that simple!

Archangels are the management, organising where and when the teams of angels under them need to go and what they should do. There is some debate as to how many archangels there are. Catholicism refers to seven, the Kabbalah (Jewish tradition) tells us there are twelve whilst other spiritual teachers say that there are fifteen or more. With humanity in such a state of turmoil at the moment, the more the better to help the world as a whole as well as helping us individually.

It is likely that each person will feel attracted to some archangels more than others, and I personally only work with three on a regular basis. It is my belief, though, that we don't need to know their names and characteristics to work with them or receive their help. By simply asking for help, they will come. And we should always ask as if it is already done; for example, "Thank you, angels, for helping me feel safe."

This is a form of prayer and, as the angels themselves transcend religion, so do prayers. Prayer is a way of connecting to the Source or Spirit of the universe, a way of expressing our intentions and having a stronger and more meaningful relationship with the unseen realms. We trust that a 'higher power', whatever we believe that to be, has heard us and is helping us to achieve our goals.

Angels can help with many different aspects of our lives, from finding a lost object to finding a parking space, from bringing us new ideas and opportunities to healing our bodies. On the other hand, we must realise that we have all signed up for our experiences so asking for healing, for example, may make things easier to deal with but may not cure us. Importantly, angels can help to resolve issues we may have with other people, so our guardian angel may have a word with another person's guardian angel, seeking a good resolution.

Problems arise, of course, because we have free will and don't always heed the advice we are given! Sometimes, we are so focused on forcing what we want to happen that we don't even hear it. We miss the subtle nudges from our bodies and minds, suggesting that we should do or not do certain things. This is when things can get messy.

It's Archangel Raphael I turn to for healing. During the spiritual circles that I hold, we send distant healing for people whom we know or have been told about needing extra help, people who are unwell or grieving or just facing a difficult period in their lives. We draw Raphael close by praying for him and imagining his emerald green light surrounding us or the person who needs help, asking him together with his healing angels help all those in our healing book.

There are times when we don't have direct and specific permission from a person in need to send healing because, for example, they may be unconscious or in the last stages of life. (It is my belief that even if someone is dying, a simple prayer to the angels will help them transition smoothly.) This also applies to the healing of small children or animals. In such circumstances, we pray "for the highest good of all, under the Law of Grace, for their growth as souls." This is a kind of direct line to the soul. We don't want to interfere with anyone's free will, so it's up to the soul whether or not they accept the healing.

During space clearing work, I always call on Archangel Michael, known as the warrior angel of protection and strength. He is often thought of as having a beautiful blue aura and a golden sword of light.

During our lives we create many energy cords, a bit like umbilical cords of energy, that can trap us and tie us to things and people that are not in our best interests. For example, if we replay a difficult memory in our mind over and over so that it just will not go away, then we have an energetic cord to that. Such cords can really hold us back, making it difficult for us to move on or making it hard for a property to sell. That is how powerful our energy is, literally tying us to situations we don't want to be in.

Archangel Michael uses his sword to cut away all negative energetic cords from people and properties, making us feel safe and protected. In space clearing, he cuts the energy cords that are holding people and spirits to that place. He helps us to move past fear and removes any fearful projections we may have placed on a property without realising we have done it.

Metatron is the other archangel who works through me when space clearing. It is believed that he is one of the few angels that was once human, known as the prophet and scribe Enoch in the Bible, and it is said that he gathered so much knowledge of the Divine that when he left his body he ascended to archangel status. He really helps us with all the changes we are going through, as a planet and a species, at this time.

During space clearing, he uses his magenta light and sacred geometry (the use of ancient symbols and shapes associated with the Divine) to clear the energy of properties. Certainly for my work, I believe he is one of the most powerful archangels.

There is also another group available to help us, the 'lightkeepers', who are highly enlightened beings come to help humanity much like the angels do. These beings will often have had a human life in which they achieved great knowledge and helped others, leading them to ascend to this important role. In the ranks, I believe, we find religious figures like Jesus, who comes to help us learn forgiveness, and his mother Mary, who brings love, faith and peace to those who call on her.

We also find gods from all religions here such as Krishna, who helps us develop and devote ourselves to spiritual practices. My personal favourite is Lord Ganesh, the Hindu elephant-head god (much loved by taxi drivers in India who believe he helps them navigate the crazy traffic there!). He works to remove any obstacles that are standing in the way of the greatest good, the perfect guide for me to work with during space clearing as he clears any blockages to the sale of a property while bringing light and infinite abundance to the place.

What about spirit guides? We can connect with them during our dreams or mediation, which is exactly how I met my spirit guide for the first time. He is a short being who wears a brown, hooded cloak, and I have never seen his face. Somehow, he reminds me of the Star Wars character Yoda (even though I am not a fan, have never watched any of the films all the way through and don't know anything about the character apart from his appearance). He certainly has a sense of humour because when I asked his name he said, "You can call me Yoda."

He is always there even when I don't want him to be, sometimes silent, sometimes really loud, but always loving and compassionate. Sometimes he randomly whispers in my ear and gives me information for people or guides me on my next step. He will even use others, like my husband Barry, to say something that triggers a message, as though he has a magic wand that activates things when I am not supposed to be working.

Anyone who does spiritual work, I feel, has a responsibility to respect others, their beliefs and their personal space, so I will never go up to anyone and give them a message unless I know them or they have asked me to. Yoda understands that of course, but once in a blue moon he will share something with me to test my ethics…

During my space clearing work, I feel it is more that the angels and lightkeepers work through me rather than I work with them. I call on Archangel Michael, Archangel Metatron and Lord Ganesh by name, and also ask for any angels and guides that can help to come in. I have one hundred per cent trust in the information that comes through even when it makes no sense to me; it often doesn't but always does to my client. I also trust whatever I see, even though some things seem unbelievable and, if I hadn't seen them with my own eyes, I would have thought them impossible.

Another difficult aspect of my spiritual work that requires faith is timing, because time is very much of the physical world and, let's face it, we've all got used to wanting things to happen immediately if not yesterday. My clients and I need to have faith in 'divine timing', that everything will unfold at the perfect time and for the highest good.

For example, as you will read later, for most properties that have been struggling things will move really fast. But there are still occasions when a property is a bit more niche, or overpriced, or there are tricky external factors, and even after space clearing they do not fly out of the door. Nonetheless, these properties are always much happier, calmer and more attractive to buyers.

4

THE HOUSE OF HORRORS

I had done an oracle card reading for a client – I'll call her Gill. While we were chatting later, she said she had a problem with her house and asked if I would be able to help. When I arrived, even the outside seemed dark and uninviting, the total opposite of Gill's personality.

I started with the bathroom. One reason for this was that there was no way I could go to the loo without first clearing the energy! The second reason was that Gill's dog wouldn't go anywhere near the room and would cry if the door was shut, which meant that the family had to bathe with the door open even when there were friends staying. It was not nice. I saw immediately that before it was a bathroom it had been used as a room to hold children in, and what these kids went through was unimaginable, horrific.

What happened as I cleared the space, by clapping and burning sage and palo santo, was something I had never experienced before and it frightened Gill. As I was telling her about a man with dark energy, a portly, grey and evil man, my face started to change. I could feel it being pulled down and she could see it. Personally, I wasn't scared as I could also see the army of angels in a circle of bright white silhouettes around me and I knew, without question, that they were keeping me safe.

Once I was sure the dark man had gone and all the residual pain, anger and terror had been removed, I carried on with the clearing using my bells and singing bowl. As I went around the house, more amazing things started to happen. In one room Gill suddenly said, "Your eyes are shining so brightly, and you look like you are shining, your whole body is glowing." The angels were working really hard on this house!

The house was on a hill and had two entrances, one for an apartment and one for the main house above it. We next moved down to the ground floor apartment and this had the same kind of energy as the bathroom upstairs, uncomfortable and troubled. Gill's friend had been with us until now, but she point-blank refused to go any further.

As I worked, I saw a priest and knew that he'd been collaborating with the man from upstairs, then had a falling out because they were both greedy, selfish and evil men. They committed a lot of crimes together, theft, rape and even murder. The priest had used the church as a cover story although not very successfully as the villagers knew what he was up to but were all scared. As I worked and moved him away, the place became noticeably lighter; Gill couldn't believe it, saying it was just like someone had turned a light switch on.

It took me seven hours to clear that house and it's fair to say I was thoroughly exhausted by the time I'd finished, but the results were better than I could have hoped for. Gill emailed me later to say that everyone who entered the house could not believe the difference. She had finished an artistic commission that she'd been unable to do before and business was now booming. Her neighbours, who were related to the previous owner and had been causing a lot of problems with fighting and being threatening towards her, had totally calmed down and even started saying hello to her rather than shouting abuse.

The really surprising thing for us both was that, without changing her diet, she had lost the weight she'd been struggling with since moving into the house. This was an extreme situation and it shows the huge effect that negative energies can have on the people who live with them.

I was asked to help a friend sell her house as it had been on the market for two and a half years, she had fallen out with the estate agent and thought that between us we may be able to sell it privately. At the property, I did a card reading for her as she was unsure which path to take.

There were two spirits nearby, which is not unusual when I am doing a reading. Actually, I had spent quite a lot of time in this property over the years and the same two spirits were always present and never troublesome. The next day, I went to space clear and the spirits had gone; there was no residual information. Nothing. I carried on anyway and programmed the house to sell quickly and for the perfect buyers to be happy, healthy and abundant in their new home.

It worked. Within a week, an estate agent who had done a valuation but hadn't been instructed, sold the house and a large deposit was paid. It just shows that even when energies are not noticeably negative they can still be holding a property back. It's those energy cords.

What does programming the property mean? Basically, I set the intention that any problems should be resolved, calling on the angels to do this and trusting that they will ensure the property is filled with light energy and that that negative or dark energy cannot enter. I ask the angels to take any earthbound spirits to the light so that they can continue their souls' growth. And I always ask that the property is filled with happiness, health and abundance, for the highest good of all.

If a property is for sale, I ask that it sells quickly, easily and well for the benefit of all and that the new owners are happy in their new home. If there are legal issues or business problems, I ask for these to be resolved in the best interests of all parties. All of this is done with prayer and with the highest intentions. When I clear remotely with a floor plan, I write the programming onto the plan and say a prayer.

Programming was especially important at a certain mountain village house, miles from anywhere and full of history. The surrounding hills and mountains were filled with tunnels and I got the feeling that this had been a place of escape since well before the Civil War here in Spain. The house was about two hundred years-old and still kept much of its original charm.

The owner was in fact very aware of energy and had already done a lot of space clearing work themselves. However, the place was full of residual energy so there were still more layers to uncover. I started at the top and, in a bedroom, I straight away saw a young woman in her twenties from around the time the house was built. The information I received was that she was in labour but the child had died, and the young woman was unable to have other children as a result.

But there was more. Fascinatingly, this woman was actually the current owner of the property in a past life. She told me now that she had always believed she was unable to have children, which I hadn't known before the clearing.

I moved on to the lounge which had an odd area above the stairs, the width of a corridor with a drop over the stairs, where I could see a lady and a child hiding in the corner. It felt like this area had once been closed off as a hiding place and, in fact, the whole house had a feeling of hiding and escaping about it. When I moved downstairs, I came across more energy of escaping.

In the summer lounge there was a very odd situation. A spirit seemed to be just lying in front of the fireplace and he told me that this was where he was buried, before the house was built. I moved him on and the room became warmer straight away. In a cupboard under the stairs, a boy of about seven years of age was hiding; but this was residual energy, not an earthbound spirit.

I came to the real source of the energy cords in the kitchen, which was at the front of the house with a doorway out to a narrow village street. Here I saw lots of activity, with people being hidden in different areas of the house or shown straight to a tunnel. My feeling was that this was once a kitchen supplying the whole village with food, maybe a bakery or something similar. But the business was not commercial, it was for getting people out and away. It might well have been a halfway safe house throughout its history, for people escaping the persecution of the Spanish Inquisition and then, later, the Civil War.

In the basement there was a window that was bricked up, and I can only guess it belonged to the same room as a blocked door I found in the garden. Personally, I would have unbricked it to see what was there as I do know it's nothing bad. Down here had been the tunnel. It was covered up now but just a few metres of digging would show it. I loved working in this house with such a colourful and interesting history.

I referred above to a past life. Have we lived before? In my experience, yes, we have; I have some past life memory and so for me it is not even a question. However, I realise that most people do not have those memories. We are in a time of 'the great forgetting'. For most of us, when we are born all our past life memories are forgotten.

Having said that, those lives can have a huge impact on how we experience this lifetime. Have you even been to a place that you have not visited before yet you just known your way around, or met a person you feel like you know, even though you have never met them before? It was like that when I met my husband; we just knew each other and we knew that the adventure of this lifetime would be taken together. Fears and phobias, as well as illnesses and addictions, can sometimes be linked to past lives and, indeed, can be healed by regression therapy.[2]

---

[2] Do read *Past Life Healing* by Judy Sharp (Local Legend, 2022), a national prize-winning book that explores beliefs and evidence regarding reincarnation. It includes many case studies of people being healed of illness or phobia by past life regression therapy.

Another country house had me puzzled for a while. It had been a home filled with kindness despite life there not always being easy, with times of hard work, struggle and poverty. Yet the energies of love and kindness were so strong that they outweighed the difficulties.

The kitchen had once been an animal shed and home to a very hardworking donkey. The dining room was originally the kitchen with a large fireplace, sadly long gone, used for cooking. The room retained some original features including the very strong memory of a large, short, smiley woman who was always cooking and caring for the men. She had been happy and had enjoyed looking after all the men, her husband and three sons plus other workers, many of whom had just been passing through when they came in from the fields.

However, the hallway had the heaviest energy of the whole house and I was unable to pinpoint why. And the downstairs bedroom, now being used as an office, had a very heavy and dark energy, the memory of a woman who had died during a miscarriage bringing sadness and loss. I recommended that the owner put a rose quartz crystal on the desk to help bring the energy of love back into the room. The lounge, which was connected to the office, was also being affected by the woman's energy.

The bathroom had been a food store. In the late nineteenth century, the occupants of the house had hidden a man in here to keep him safe from the police, who were acting on behalf of the Church. When they came, they searched for him but he successfully escaped over the mountain at the back of the property.

In the main bedroom, the energy was a little unstable so I recommended that the owners put an amethyst on the bedside table along with something in the far corner, such as a tall lamp or large crystal or something hanging from ceiling. These things would help to balance the energy of the room.

Upstairs in the first bedroom was a visiting spirit girl, Carmen. In a white dress and with long, dark brown hair in bunches, she just wanted to play with the child who now lived in the house. She had died suddenly of a fever in the early twentieth century. There was no harm in her, but I helped her to move on as, in this case, it was the right thing to do.

The second bedroom upstairs was really dark, heavy and negative. I could not get any information as to why but it was very uncomfortable. I recommended that the owner turned the horseshoes the right way up so that good fortune stayed in the house instead of flowing away. (If you have horseshoes in your home, make sure the 'legs' are facing upwards!)

Finally, I programmed the house to be happy, calm, healthy and abundant in every way, for the children to do well at school, and for any and all businesses that are run from there to be hugely successful and profitable.

Did anything I have said make sense to the owner? She later confirmed that she had been unable to work in her office because of feeling very uncomfortable there, but now she felt relaxed and had been able to be productive in that space. She had also spoken to her daughter and asked if she ever had friends that Mummy didn't know come to play. The girl answered no, but she would like to know who the ghost was that often played with her! Her mother had not known about Carmen before then. The family are now thriving and living very happily in their lovely country home.

I was asked to clear another property by a member of one of my spiritual circle groups. There were no major problems, she just wanted to experience space clearing and see if it would make her home feel even more comfortable. She had a lot of cats who were very interested in what I was doing and watched me the whole time! The overall energies of the home were calm and good, just like its owners'.

In the lounge I was shown a memory of a large, short woman,

dressed in black. She was cooking on the fire and she suffered from headaches. It was a hard life but a happy one. The bathroom was once a storage area and had the energetic imprint of a little boy hiding from his father. The kitchen had been at one point an animal shed and had a lovely calm, heart-of-the-home sort of energy. The main bedroom was calm and peaceful, like a sanctuary and a very pleasant space to be in.

But the downstairs bedroom had a much heavier feeling than the rest of the house. And I felt a pressure on my chest especially when I went into the ensuite bathroom. It was like a dark cloud hung over these two rooms, very different to the rest of the house. There was a breathlessness feeling here and the rooms were physically colder.

A spirit man called Antonio was there. He was short and very skinny and brought sadness and illness with him. He smoked homemade cigarettes, which the owner confirmed she had smelled. Once I had cleared the home and sent Antonio on his way, the owner reported that she was very glad she had asked me do the work. She and her daughter felt a big difference. Their relationship had become stronger and the home seemed more full of love than it had before.

Another friend also asked me to space clear his property, not because there were any issues but he was intrigued to find out what secrets his home had to tell. He had moved from one of the Spanish islands with his two teenage daughters, and with a very clear vision of what their family home would look like. Indeed, he had spent a long time finding it. It was a *cortijo*, or farm house, just off a *rambla*, a dry river bed. Remote yet accessible, you could walk to the nearest town from it but you would never find it if you didn't know it was there.

It had everything he wanted except that it only had one bedroom. The plan was to put two yurts on the land for the girls, which would be a wonderful and imaginative solution to the space problem.

As I cleared the house I found only imprinted energy, that of an old couple and a donkey. They had been escaping persecution in the 1930s, which was common in this area of Spain, and had lived in a cave while they lovingly built their home. The present owner had not found a cave but did say that, according to the previous owner, some of the hillside behind the house had been removed so it was possible that there had been a cave there. The old couple had lived happily in the house until their deaths, the husband going first and then closely followed by his heartbroken wife.

The house was then inherited by a family member and had become a party house, something that is commonplace in Spain when families inherit a *cortijo* and use it just for family parties. Growing up myself in a family that would often gather and party with no excuse needed, I love that idea. Because of this, and the quiet nature of the old couple, the energy of this home was beautifully peaceful, full of fun and love. I did still call in the angels to remove any negativity, just to be one hundred per cent sure that all would be great for this lovely family.

Later, I was honoured to return having been asked to teach the eldest daughter how to space clear. Her yurt had arrived! She is a very spiritually aware and connected young woman with an aura that lights up a room, and I wanted to help her stay that way.

As with houses and objects, yurts can of course also hold energy. We set about clearing it, with me showing her what to do and then she would copy me. As we went along, I asked her what she could sense, helping her to connect to her natural ability. There wasn't much to report apart from some sadness, which was easy to dispel. I am delighted to say that she has since space cleared for one of her friend's parents, as well as giving them an oracle card reading. She is a very powerful spiritual being and I cannot wait to help and encourage her to do the amazing work that is her purpose in this lifetime. She is going to bring so much light and positivity to the world, it's exciting to watch.

5

DARK SECRETS

C uevas del Almanzora (*cuevas* means caves) is a town filled with history and grand buildings and dates back to the Bronze Age. Its castle, Marquis de los Vélez, was the first fortification at this site and probably originally an Arabic defensive watchtower of the late 13th or early 14th century; the present structure was built in the first half of the 16th century.

The castle has an irregular rectangular layout and inside its walls are a former palace of the Marquis and a keep that probably incorporated the older Arabic tower. Inside there is also a fortified warehouse where taxes would have been collected and stored, especially important after silver was discovered in the previously agricultural land nearby, bringing riches and reputation to the town. The mines have long since gone, mainly because they kept flooding in the late 1800s and became too expensive to operate, but the grandeur of the town's architecture is still noticeably visible along many of its narrow roads. Nowadays, the various buildings inside the restored castle house a museum, a library and a police station.

The rich history of the town goes a long way to explaining the amazing properties I have had the honour to space clear there. One of these is El Palacete, within view of the castle and situated just below it in the town hall square. With so many stories surrounding it, along with the second largest religious building in the whole province, Iglesia de la Encarnacion, at the corner of the road, it is no great surprise that the beautiful El Palacete had many hidden secrets to share.

It is now a stunning 19th century rural boutique guesthouse with seven ensuite rooms and when I was introduced to the co-owner I had no idea what an amazing friendship and working relationship would unfold. Ellie and I had an instant connection, as though our souls have met many times over many lifetimes.

Ellie was arranging for public talks to take place there and she was keen to meet up and see what I was doing. That first day, we booked in a talk and then she asked if I would space clear the guesthouse. What a privilege that was. We now work together regularly running day retreats, calling ourselves 'Alchemy Retreats'. The hotel is about to expand and, when renovations are complete on the property next door, I shall space clear that too. I'm sure there will be many stories to be told and a few spirits hiding in there.

El Palacete itself certainly had hidden secrets even though the energy had been changed hugely due to the love and respect it had been shown during renovations. As I entered, I was greeted by a spirit lady who told me her name was Rose, although she was clearly Spanish. It turned out her name was Rosa. I find it fascinating that Spanish spirits always communicate with me in English, even though I speak their language. I guess spirits will always communicate with us in the easiest way for us to understand, or perhaps our minds automatically do a translation. Anyway, language is no longer a barrier to the spirit worlds.

Sometimes, instead, they show pictures in the mind's eye. During oracle card readings, if a client is in some sort of turmoil I will often be shown a washing machine drum going round and round!

Rosa informed me that she was 'the gatekeeper', making sure that nothing negative could enter the property. She also said that she was loosely connected to the owner, who may not even remember her. When the owner had first moved to the area, they used to greet each other as they passed in the street, nothing more than that. But Rosa was so impressed by the young lady and what she was doing with El Palacete that she had taken it upon herself to protect them both!

If you should ever visit, do say hello to Rosa. She's sitting in the entrance in an old rocking chair and loves nothing more than being acknowledged.

As I moved through the hotel, however, the energy changed and before long I was confronted by an angry priest. He was very upset that I was there, standing in front of me shouting that I was doing "the devil's work". Interestingly, he was very much stuck in one particular area and it appeared that Rosa was preventing his access to the rest of the building, although she could do no more than that. Indeed, it even took me a while to move him on, but he no longer brings his negative and bullying energy into the place.

In a small corner, which at some time would have been part of a corridor, there was the memory of a young boy cowering against the wall and I got the strong feeling that he was hiding from the priest I had just encountered. Many years ago, the properties on this site would probably have been strongly attached to the Church and the boy may well have been some sort of servant.

As I moved upstairs, there were no other spirits, just memory imprints. In one room there was a lady dressed in white, standing by the window and crying. She was waiting for her son to return, having been taken from her to join the Church. The next area had a well-to-do lady wearing what appeared to be very expensive clothes of the period when the house had just been built. My impression was that she had fallen into financial hardship; furniture and jewellery were being sold in order for her to keep up appearances. It was a sad scene, one of non-acceptance.

As I moved to the bedrooms, the information coming through to me changed. A young woman in one room wanted me to pass a message on to the owner saying how wonderfully the property had been renovated and how much she appreciated all the care and attention to detail that had gone into this place. She was just passing through, not a fixture to the building. But other information I received was actually from furniture rather than from spirits or the building itself. An ancient chest of drawers, for example, showed me babies sleeping soundly in its bottom drawer and brought a feeling of calm and peace to the room.

By contrast, a four-poster bed showed a large bully of a man who seemed to have aspired to be like Henry VIII – fat, bad-mannered and selfish beyond belief. He died from his 'excesses' in the bed. Then there was a woman in childbirth who also died in this bed. I felt that the bed had been unused for a number of years, maybe even decades, and Ellie later confirmed this.

In case you're thinking of visiting, I can assure you that the bed is now clear of all the negative energy and, as with every room and bed in the property, is programmed to give the best night's sleep to all who lay their heads on the pillows. In fact, I have now had the privilege to sleep in the four-poster bed myself, a treat to celebrate my birthday and our wedding anniversary. I would not have been able to do that if I had not space cleared it, and Ellie is not surprised when her guests tell her they have had the best night's sleep ever.

The last bedroom I investigated had a darker feel about it and it became clear that the energy was coming from a prayer stool in the corner of the room. This was imprinted with the memory of young boys being hit around the head with a Bible. There was that darkness of priests and Church again, leaving an atmosphere that emanated fear and anger.

There was a self-contained apartment attached to the guesthouse, which had recently been under renovation. It had a separate entrance and the guesthouse was beside and also above it. The apartment was bursting with character and had been lovingly renovated to the same high standard as the main guesthouse.

But its energy was very different, full of sadness, violence and desperation. The first time I saw it, I found it a difficult space to be in. Yes, it really needed space clearing and the results, I'm happy to say, have been noticed by all who entered before and after. So why was the energy so heavy in this particular area of the hotel? As I entered, it became clear to me that this property had been divided up and rented out, some people having a few rooms, some having just one. So not only was there complicated residual energy, there were also earthbound spirits and not just one or two.

The energy was thick from the very start of the hallway. I saw a woman being dragged out of the building by her hair, perhaps around the 1930s. She was angry about being unjustly treated, wrongly accused of being a witch. (I am relieved they don't still do that because I'm sure I would be on the list!) In the first area I came to, a family had lived in two rooms at the beginning of the twentieth century. The energy was all residual but uncomfortable even so. I saw a mother crying, rocking a little girl around four years-old as they huddled in a corner. Then the image of a man appeared – I heard the name Juan. He was a violent and dark energy in life and had left that imprint on the property. He had caused his wife multiple miscarriages due to his violent nature and pain and suffering were his legacy.

Further into the apartment was a one-room bedsit whose occupant had been a very depressed and lonely woman. I think her name was Encarna. She had been forced into prostitution just to stay alive and the pain and sadness in her space was huge, although she did not work out of the room. All around this area of the apartment was fear, sorrow and, again, hiding.

At the rear of the apartment, I came across a brave family. Diego, his wife Rosa (a different one) and their young son, Pepe. They were anti-Fascist and stood up for what they believed in. Diego himself had dug an escape tunnel here, which is now filled in and made into a feature wall. The tunnel area itself was unpleasant, the energy thick and heavy with fear and terror. I struggled for breath, finding myself really wanting to cry.

There were also six spirits stuck in the space: three women, two men and a child around nine years-old. They were stuck because of what had happened to them here. As they had tried to escape through the tunnel, they had been cornered and shot, their bodies falling on top of each other and left to rot. The boy, still alive but injured, was buried underneath the other bodies. Diego, Rosa and Pepe were among the dead.

Yet Diego clearly got the message across to me that he would do it all again. He was determined that what he was fighting for was right. The other two women and man, though, felt cheated and wrongly accused. I kept hearing, "We did not steal." They had been set up, someone had informed on them, and the Guardia Civil had been waiting for them at the tunnel. The authorities of that time, the late 1930s, had no compassion or remorse. It was almost like a game to them.

At the other end of the tunnel I saw a priest, overlooking the shooting and enjoying the show. He enjoyed the destruction, fear and pain. He would tell people not to cross him because he was "doing God's work", but he was only serving himself because he liked the control and power that the Church offered him at that time. All those poor souls have now been taken to the light and it is my hope they will find peace.

I have learned that this was a very important tunnel that had helped almost one hundred people escape from the priests and Guardia Civil, who were acting in support of Fascism and, later, Franco. It was used mainly before the Civil War, as people tried to escape the inevitable, although there was serious political unrest in Spain from the late 1920s until the dictator Franco died in 1975. In those days there were escape tunnels in many properties and in fact the new part of El Palacete has another one.

This leads me to believe that the people of this town were brave, with strong values and morals in the face of personal danger every day. These good souls selflessly protected others, and the 'tunnels of hope' should not be forgotten. They are a reminder to us all that we sometimes have to stand up and say, "No more." And that justice and goodness will overcome evil eventually.

Today, the owners of El Palacete have named all the rooms after local women and have created a back story for them that hangs outside each door. There is also a story for Rosa, the friendly gatekeeping spirit, placed in the entrance of the building.

I had the privilege of being asked to space-clear another mansion in Cuevas, El Palacete Villanita, a truly amazing place with a long and interesting history. At the time it was being rented out as a holiday let and was on the market for two and half million euros.

Due to its size, I was going to clear it in two parts and the night before starting the work information was already coming through to me. I was shown the house and garden around the eighteenth century with a tall Arabic man standing very proudly by the front door. Strangely, I then saw Chatsworth House, in Derbyshire, UK, which has been occupied by the Cavendish family since it was built in the mid-sixteenth century. Perhaps one building inspired the architecture of the other or there were other family connections.

I began in the hallway. Clearly, this had been a very important place with rich and powerful people staying from all over the world and attending big parties, political and business meetings. There was the strong energy of jealousy. Right by the front door was a walking stick with a cross on it and there was another identical cross on a plaque in the lounge. These crosses had come from a monastery, which had left an imprint of negative energy that would keep resurfacing like a curse. Even though I cleared the items individually, this kind of energy was never going to be banished entirely so I encouraged the owner to get them out of the house.

In the piano room was a beautiful picture of a graveyard. However, it was bringing a feeling of anger and grief with it, so I spent some time clearing it. The piano itself held the memory of a young girl being forced to practise for hours and hours.

The next area was being used as an office and lounge where I sensed an overwhelming feeling of dizziness and sickness, as though life was a struggle to get through. There was also the residual energy of an old man who was stubborn, lonely and ill. I even saw him throwing up blood, which was very unpleasant. He spent most of his time in these rooms.

This part of the building also had the energy of soldiers passing through, laughing and joking, many of them from different times wearing different uniforms, some dating back to before the house was built.

Venturing upstairs I came to what were originally three small servant rooms, now partly converted into a bathroom and walk-in wardrobe. This was thick and heavy with sadness. I saw a child, only about three or four years-old, locked in the small loft cupboard. He was the son of the owner and his nanny had locked him in as a warning of what would happen if he didn't respect her.

Thankfully I was greeted by a much nicer scene back downstairs in the hallway and back bedroom, where there were happy children running, laughing and playing hide and seek. Lovely energy here, unlike the front part of the house. As I moved into another bedroom, I came across more soldiers from perhaps the nineteenth century in what felt like some sort of boot room. Interestingly, all the energy in the dining room was coming from a beautiful old mirror, bringing uncertainty and confusion. It had seen so much that it had held onto its own memories. I cleared it so that it could now shine with its true beauty.

Throughout much of the work, I could tell that someone was following and watching me and, as I entered the kitchen, I came face to face with him. He was a spirit man who did not like people being there! Pepe was from around the late nineteenth century and was connected to other spirits on the lower floor. I moved him on. The owners later confirmed that they had always felt uncomfortable in the kitchen and, like me, had that sense of being watched. They also actively avoided going downstairs because of the energy there.

But I couldn't put it off any longer. As I walked downstairs I saw a gecko on the floor. In many cultures around the world, geckos and lizards are considered to be good luck and protectors, with many homes in Spain, including mine, having ceramic or metal geckos on their walls. They are said to be courageous creatures, intrepid and adventurous with a passion for life and the ability to enjoy it. Unfortunately, my cat thinks they are a delicacy.

I took this particular gecko as a very positive sign that I was protected in this amazing building.

The lower floor of the mansion was basically a blank canvas, split into two halves with separate entrances. The back half overlooked a still beautiful, walled garden, complete with a swimming pool and a banana tree with a healthy crop of fruit. Although the garden was not very well maintained at the moment, it was bustling with the energy of days gone by, of relaxation and enjoyment.

This was in contrast to the downstairs of this house, which had a very heavy feeling about it. Again, I came across soldiers but this time they were marching. Next I encountered two spirit men. The first was the same tall Arab I had seen the night before I began the clearing. It was his house. He was an important and rich merchant and he did not like so many other people in his house or understand why it had changed so much. He knew he was dead, but still thought things should have stayed the same. There was also a shorter man giving off an angry air of entitlement.

The whole area felt stuck, almost as though time had stood still. Even though this part of the property had been stripped and some renovation work had clearly been done, the two spirits were not helping the stuck feeling. As I moved through to the back,

I saw that it had once been a stunning summer lounge with the best lavish furnishings of its day, with a wonderful reading room with the most amazing, relaxed energy, some of which remained.

Suddenly the strangest thing happened, which could have been terrifying if I had not had my wits about me. I was confronted by a large, black dog with rabies, like something out of a horror film, snarling and foaming at the mouth. It showed itself much larger than a dog would be, in fact larger than me, and I understood that it was just the way this spirit animal wanted to be viewed because he was a guard dog. He was there to protect the property and its owners and didn't know he was dead, so had been trying to do his job for well over a hundred years.

Once again, I had the feeling of being watched. This time it was a priest and I was shown insights into his life. He had watched what happened in the house with great interest, jealous of the wealth the owners had. He felt this was unfair so he would blackmail them for what he felt were unholy activities. He did give some of the money to the Church but pocketed a sizeable amount for himself.

The energy was very masculine all around this area, almost as though very few women had lived there. In fact, the whole of the property felt very masculine.

There was a bedroom with its own entrance via the garden where I met a stern spirit man. He had the air of a butler about him, wanting everything to be done properly. I couldn't tell whether he was Spanish but I would say he had definitely been trained in England because he had that characteristic stiff upper lip! He didn't want to leave as no-one else could do the work the way it should be done. Moreover, he was not happy that the mansion was no longer a hive of parties and important guests, as it once had been. I moved him on to his soul's next adventure.

The front part of the lower floor was very interesting and I could see that once upon a time there had been an amazing entrance hall and staircase, sadly now long gone. In fact, there was no direct access upstairs here. The original door was dark, heavy wood and with very impressive, beautiful carvings. But the overall feeling in this part of the building was sadness, that it had never been used to its full potential.

Residual energy from before the house was built was still evident. The land had housed a military hospital and the associated pain and suffering still echoed in the land and, in turn, the property. This may have been why this downstairs area had never been used as originally intended – it was just not a comfortable place to be in. There was little direct sunlight here, although the light coming in through the large, glass-panelled front door had kept the negative energy at bay and helped to clear some of the past trauma the area had witnessed.

The whole area had a strange energy, like the building itself was crying out for a purpose, to be used and enjoyed. I felt dizzy, with a sense of confusion. The lower part of this magnificent building was a blank canvas and indeed would make a fantastic space for an art gallery, museum or social venue. There was plenty of room for a restaurant too. I am told that there had been plans for something like that but, for unknown reasons, the idea never grew wings. Perhaps the butler and the guard dog had something to do with it…

It was not a great surprise to me to find so much information and so many spirits in this most remarkable building. I never know what I am going to find when I space clear and this one definitely did not disappoint. I released all the spirits and sent them to the light, free to continue their souls' journeys. I also hope my work will help this unique property to find new owners with great vision (and deep pockets) to honour its amazing history.

You may be wondering why so many priests have turned up in these accounts. Well, Spanish history is packed with priests, so it is no surprise that I am often confronted by them while space clearing. They are normally not pleased to meet me and, for my part, it has to be said that they are invariably among the most unpleasant spirits I have come across.

They like to come really close to me – as close as my spirit guides and angels will allow – and get right up in my face. They call me an "evil witch" and are just downright threatening and aggressive.

I guess this is not a huge surprise, due to the Church's history of violence and abuse, especially dating back to the Spanish Inquisition that was established in 1478 and executed some five thousand people over the next three centuries. Added to that was the Church's support for Franco during the Civil War. There were many priests who used their authority for their own gain and whose daily activities had little or nothing to do with God.

Thankfully, that reign of terror seems to have ended in more recent times, the Church offering comfort and support to those who attend. Modern priests appear to be genuine 'men of God' although I'm sure there are some exceptions. But the spirit priests I have come across have been far from that, without exception hiding behind religion to allow them to do whatever they wanted. These evil men from times gone by were responsible for torture, extortion and any other atrocity you can think of including murder.

So why is it that, even as spirits, the priests I come across are still evil? One reason may be that they are earthbound, never having actually believed in a spiritual afterlife. But moreover, even in death, the need to have control and power persists. The minds of such people are full of insecurity, of anger and fear. And as spirits, they still have the power to impact others negatively.

Very often, a property becomes noticeably lighter once I have space cleared and these spirits have moved on. I feel truly blessed to be able to bring more harmony to this world, even in a small way, one property at a time.

6

EVERYTHING CHANGES!

After a friend, and the owner of one of the houses I had space cleared, saw that I was doing the work as a business with amazing results, she contacted me with an intriguing suggestion. She had a problem with one of her tenants and didn't know what to do because she couldn't get access. Could I help to clear the issue from a picture and a floor plan if I knew the address too? I had never done anything like this before and had no idea if it was possible, but I was willing to give it a go.

As I studied the plan, the information started to arrive. It was evident that, yes, I could do it. Now, this was a game-changer!

This is how it works. I ask the client to send me a very basic layout of the property, not necessarily to scale. If the property is on the market, though, the client will already have a floor plan that their estate agent has done. I then protect myself spiritually and open myself up to receive information by visualising a door opening at my third eye (in the centre of the forehead) enabling me to see clearly; I also visualise light coming from my ears so I can hear clearly, and a door opening at my heart to receive and give unconditional love.

Now imagine a dial at the back of the head, like an old-fashioned radio dial: with this I 'tune in' to the angels and guides, in order to receive the information I need. Once all that is done,

I redraw the plans by hand which helps me to tune in to the energy of the property. (There has been one exception to this rule and that was when I was asked to space clear a van! My artistic skills are not up to drawing a van, so I concentrated on a photo of the vehicle instead.) I write the property address on the top of the page so that my angels and guides are in no doubt which property we are working on, although to be fair I think they already know.

Next I place the plans on a table in my office along with crystals I have cleansed and charged in the same way as described earlier. I ask for the crystals to help me clear the energy of the property as I place them around the plans together with candles (I like to use two Himalayan pink salt tealight holders) as they also help to clear negative energy and, I believe, have health benefits. No, there is no scientific evidence for this, yet many people do report that sleep disorders, anxiety and even depression have been improved by using salt lamps. They also look very pretty!

Calling in the angels and guides, I thank them for all the information I shall receive and for clearing any energy that is not serving the property or its occupants. I clap over the plans and use Palo Santo and sage, just as I do when space clearing in person.

This is when information normally starts to come in. I write it all down in order to compile a report for my client, then use my bells and singing bowls to clear the property. This whole process is much faster than in-person clearings so at this point I go and sit quietly in another room to see if anything else needs to be shared. This works for me. I don't want to be receiving information all day about a property I have cleared earlier.

Once I have received all there is to be shared, I ask the angels and guides to clear the energy of the property further. Starting with Archangel Michael, I ask him to cut any cords that are holding the property or its occupants, past and present. Then I ask Archangel Metatron to use his sacred geometry and magenta light to cleanse the energy. If the property is on the market, I call on Lord Ganesh to removes all obstacles to the property's sale.

There's one final necessary task. If I have come across any earthbound spirits or other entities, I ask that they be taken to the light for the highest good of all. And of course I give thanks to all the angels and guides for making the property a healthy, happy and abundant home for the present or future owners.

The plans stay on my office table overnight with the crystals on them and the candles burning out naturally. I feel this helps to enhance the whole process for the best results. Because of all this, I rarely do more than one property a day.

Often, I do not have to wait long for my clients' feedback. I really love receiving this, not only when it confirms the information I have received but especially if they can feel a difference and the work has had the desired outcome. Very occasionally there is no immediate significant change so I go back and redo the space clearing. Sometimes, new information arrives or old cords have reattached. I want the best outcome for all so I will revisit a property until that is realised.

What of my friend's house with access problems? It was a lovely family home but it felt cold and sad. The tenants were shown to me as good people but carrying a lot of trauma. I cleared that energy the best I could and programmed the property to help them let go of their past pains and upsets. I also came across a spirit man, probably in his seventies, of average height but thin and looking worn-out as though he had had a heavy physical job. He was wearing a flat cap and had a 'grandad' feeling about him. The man had been earthbound – this often causes upset in a property's energy – but I was able to move him on so that his spirit was free to enjoy its next adventure.

When I came to the front room there was the most beautiful flood of happy memories, of children laughing and running around, of a Christmas party with parlour games. It was so lovely that I confess I lingered there for a while. By contrast, the bedroom at the top of the stairs had the really sad memory of a lady crying in emotional pain, but this was residual energy and not a spirit.

She was suffering the grief of the loss of a loved one. I got the names 'Fred and Maisie' but couldn't get any more information on who they had been.

I cleared the property, setting the intention for the necessary maintenance work to be carried out quickly and effectively and for the home to be filled with love, happiness and abundance. Feedback came from the owner within twenty-four hours: the ball had already started rolling and she was over the moon. So was I! I had proved, not only to her but also to myself, that I could space clear from a floor plan with amazing results. That first experience opened the doors to helping many more people with the energy in their homes.

I had a family connection to the owner of another lovely home, which was set in a wonderful semi-rural area in the south of England. While clearing this house, which also had an adjoining apartment, one of my spirit relatives 'popped in' to send their love, which I was able to pass on to other family members. The owner was very much on a spiritual path herself and had done some space clearing.

There was the residual energy of an older couple in the main house. They were happy but worried a lot about a disabled daughter who had lived in the annexe; when they could no longer care for her, they moved her to a care home. Yet the overall feeling of this house was that it was a happy home.

The owner's Dad had appeared when I had done oracle card readings for her previously, and he now appeared again. He wanted her to know that he was really proud of her and her brother and that he was also sorry for what he had put her through. He was blunt but I had to pass this on. He warned her to be careful about trusting men and to watch out for patterns she had seen in the past: as her business took off, which it would, men around her may feel threatened so she must look after herself and her money.

I programmed the house with the added intention that the apartment should always be rented out and for the owner's business to be a huge success. She reported back that the energy in the home felt even more welcoming and peaceful than before, the apartment was now almost fully booked and her business was thriving.

A property in Angel Road needed to be cleared because the owner had been trying to sell it for a long time. Although he had received offers, the sale had always fallen through at survey because of the amount of work that needed to be done. However, the owner suspected this was not the only reason. He had lived there himself with others and it had not been a happy home; he had even suffered a breakdown there.

This was indeed a factor but the main problem was a spirit named John. He was very angry and for some reason felt that the property should be his. The overall energy in the house was of despair and confusion, darkness and depression, which would most definitely affect the mental health of anyone who lived there as well as its saleability. I also picked up that at some point there had been a fire in the second bedroom, although the owner knew nothing about this.

I cleared all the residual energy remotely and set John free. Within twenty-four hours the owner contacted me to say that he had accepted an offer from a developer who was not concerned about the amount of work to be done. The sale went through, even though the survey did reveal evidence of a fire in the second bedroom. And the owner also confirmed that John had been his lodger when he lived in the house; he had been a disturbed man who did indeed believe that the house was rightfully his. The property was now clean and clear for the developer to turn it into a wonderful family home.

The Old School House was a strange and challenging building. It was essentially one room, situated in a rural Spanish hamlet, and had been empty for a number of years. There were no lurking spirits but much residual energy of anxiety and fear, of children being slapped around and punishment being used in teaching. The house had a very unstable, manic energy, like a whirlwind, and I picked up that it was in a mess.

65

Indeed, its effect on the owner was that he felt himself spinning the whole time and not getting anywhere, trying to tidy up but finding it hard because of his mental state. I cleared all the residual energy and programmed the property to be calm, happy and abundant, to feel like a safe space.

Although this was done remotely by a floor plan, I knew the owner and could soon see a change in him. He was much calmer in himself and able to work in a more positive way to fulfil his dreams of writing books and songs. I can't wait to read his work!

My clients are not always spiritual people and some are downright sceptical. One lady asked me to clear her house just because she had heard some interesting stories about it and wanted to see whether "anything came up". She was at pains to say that she didn't really believe in this sort of work… but would I do it anyway? This always makes me smile because at some level such people must believe, otherwise why would they bother? I was careful to ask her not to tell me anything about the property so I would have no preconceptions about any stories or evidence of the past she might have heard. I would be starting with a clean slate, knowing that any information I received was from a higher place than my ego or imagination. The client could then judge my work for herself.

There were two buildings involved, the main house where my client's Dad lived and a smaller annexe for her. The main house was built around the middle of the nineteenth century and still had some of the original walls. It would have been much more basic back then and life was very hard, working the land, poverty and struggle. A donkey lived on the lower floor and upstairs was open to allow the drying of meat and vegetables in the summer, ready for winter.

It had been abandoned and left derelict for some years. The overall energy here was of instability, sadness, anger and disagreement from the majority of the people who had ever lived in the house. It was layered with energy best described as having 'sharp edges'.

The annexe was very interesting. It had started life as a barn and had lots of negative imprinted energy mainly due to two children, a boy and a girl, who had been held hostage there and abused. They left behind a feeling of being terrified. The boy had escaped but not the girl. Then I was shown an image of the well… if she wasn't in the well, she was really close to it. There was also a graveyard for babies nearby on the land. I had never come across anything like that and the overall energy was of terror, loneliness and great sadness.

Despite all this darkness, my client was amazed and delighted with the information. She confirmed the ages of the properties and said she had a well that she had been struggling to get cleared out as it was so deep. It had been suggested that it would be cheaper and easier to dig another one and my report confirmed to her that this would be better, so as not to disturb the girl. The graveyard also made sense. Rumour had it that this property had at some point been 'a house of ill repute', so a graveyard full of babies would fit with that. The property was far from any village but these babies would not have been accepted in a church graveyard anyway because of their conception.

As we have seen, historic events can leave deep impressions on a property that can be felt to the present day. On the other hand, some problems have their root in the client themselves rather than the building! One lady happened on my website and asked me to space clear the house she was staying in because she had struggled to sleep properly since moving in some eighteen months earlier. I was confident that space clearing would help – but I was wrong.

The overall energy of the place was unstable, bumpy and rather anxious. I picked up that the house had either been totally changed or the energy had come from a property that was on the land in times gone by. It turned out that, yes, the property had been extensively refurbished and extended. It was very sterile and in need of some fun, so I suggested having a party to bring it back to life!

But while I was clearing I actually felt physically sick. I managed to pinpoint this feeling to an old man, Paco, who had been very ill and had died around 1920 from a stomach illness. And the sleep issues my client was suffering from were not helped by another spirit man around twenty years-old who was a disturbed individual and very angry. He accidentally killed himself and no-one came to rescue him, which was why he was so angry. I got the name Pedro and the year 1947.

As always, I cleared the stagnant energy, moved both the spirits on and filled the house with light, programming it to be healthy, happy and abundant. I also programmed it for my client to sleep well and feel energised, positive and happy.

I always check on my clients in the days and weeks following a space clearing to see how things are going and to check that I haven't missed anything. Working from a floor plan sometimes, for example, makes it easier for spirits to hide from me. After a few days there was no improvement in my client's sleep.

I repeated the clearing but could not get any more information, except that my client had a habit of using her phone in bed. (The EMF, electromagnetic field, would definitely be unhelpful.) She bought some crystals that I recommended and stopped using her phone in bed, and although her sleep was a little better it still wasn't great.

This was not a satisfactory solution for me so I arranged to give her an oracle card reading online to find out what was going on. The reading, and our conversation, were very enlightening and took us to the root cause of the problem. She had moved into the property as a stopgap, planning to be there for only two or three months. And the fact that she had now been there for eighteen months, with all her belongings still in boxes, was the real cause of all the unstable energy and lack of sleep.

She and her husband had found a few properties they wanted

to buy but these had all fallen through due to legal problems. This was causing no end of anxiety and upset, leading to the difficulty in sleeping, which then added to the stress. The cards revealed that the perfect property was indeed on its way, and it would not be long before she was on the move…

As soon as they found their forever home, sleep improved for her. The root cause was not the house but the stress of living somewhere that didn't feel like, and would never be, home. The space clearing did have a positive effect, though, and the house felt lighter, even physically brighter.

Another client also had very disturbed nights, this time because of violent nightmares that were occurring frequently. As a result my client was always tired. Interestingly, after she gave me the plans, and before I had even done the clearing, things already started to improve.

"It's like the spirits knew they were on their way out!" she said.

It felt to me as though the house had been empty for a number of years in the past, but had now been occupied for a while. The overall energy there was of confusion, anger and sadness. I came across two spirit men. One of them was short and angry; this had been his home a long time ago but I felt he'd been forced out by Franco's men.

The second man was tall and slim with a black beard. I think he was connected to my client and he was a troublemaker, causing the nightmares. In life he would seem charming until you got to know him, but in fact he was controlling, aggressive and violent. I was given the name Fredrick, or Fred, he had lived in the UK but was not of British heritage, possibly Italian. My client could not verify the name but thought it might have been an uncle, whom she hadn't known, as her Dad looked very Italian.

I also saw a man hanging, but this was not a spirit and, strangely, it didn't feel like he was connected to the house. Was it a memory that this spirit had imprinted there for my client because they were connected? Unfortunately, my client didn't know how her father had died and there was no-one she could ask. Her Dad definitely did pop in to offer love and support, though, so it could have been his way of letting me know that it was him. As you may appreciate, these things sometimes don't make sense straight away and I have to try and work them out, like an investigator. I am human, however, so there is always a margin of error.

The property also had rental apartments attached. These had been animal sheds in the past and the energy in them was pretty clear, albeit with a slight lingering feeling of deception. I think this was due to some robbers who had been caught at the apartments. As always, I cleared all the negative energy and enhanced the positive, removed all spirits and programmed the house for good sleep, profitable business and to be healthy, happy and abundant.

My client reported back that her sleep was now not disturbed by bad dreams, and this was having a positive effect on the rest of her life. The apartments were booked as much as she wanted them to be, and she had seen the difference in her home since I space cleared it.

However much I do this work, there is always something new to surprise me. Another country house also had a disturbed occupant, my client's husband! He was acting completely 'out of character'. Now, this client was a spiritual woman, well aware of space clearing and indeed she regularly cleared her property herself. She also believed in the 'evil eye' talisman and had it fixed on every entrance to her home.[3]

Unsurprisingly, the energy of the house itself was pretty clear. However, I had never before seen anything like what I was shown there – and if I hadn't seen it myself I would never have believed it possible.

---

[3] This talisman, or amulet, dates back about five thousand years and is believed to stop any malevolent curse directed towards the wearer. It is a representation of an eye, often in the form a glass bead, thought to reflect the curse back to the sender.

There was an entity attached to the man of the house. The only way I can describe it is like the monster Gollum who first appeared in J R R Tolkien's 1937 fantasy novel, *The Hobbit*, and then in its sequel, *The Lord of the Rings*. This figure was heavy and dark, with very sharp claws attached to the man's back. No wonder he was acting out of character! He must have felt like he was carrying a really heavy load, walking through treacle, with every task hard work. Nothing would feel clear, he would have felt unmotivated and stuck in a rut.

I prized Gollum off but he was not keen to leave. It left me exhausted and I knew the energetic disturbance would leave the victim feeling drained for a few days too. I ended by asking for a bubble of protection to be placed around the house and its occupants. My client confirmed that her husband had indeed felt very tired for a while but then he was back to his old self. She also told me that she had received a message from her Dad in spirit, through her Mum, saying that I had done a really good job.

It's so lovely to receive commendation from the spirit world!

7

HEALING

There was another interesting, but far more pleasant, first for me at a family home on a *rambla*. The main house's occupants were a married couple, and there was an annexe occupied by their pregnant daughter and her partner. The daughter was very psychic and the activity they were experiencing was in no small part attracted to her energy.

I started with the annexe where there was mainly residual energy of frustration and 'not being heard'. However, there was a spirit lady too, who gave her name as June. She was attached to the property, not the couple, and I felt she had lived there, the frustration of not being heard coming from her. They also had four regular spirit visitors. There was the partner's mother, the homeowner's grandmother, and a man whom the homeowner called Dad (who wanted her to know that, as far as he was ever concerned, she was his daughter and he loved her very much).

The fourth spirit visitor was especially interesting because she was the owner's mother – and she was still alive!

In my work I had never come across the visiting spirit of someone alive. Yet I do know that it is possible for souls to travel to different places while they still have a human body, because my own daughter used to do this when she was asleep as a baby. I would put her in her cot in her room and then her soul would suddenly appear by the side of my bed.

Now, the owner's mother had dementia, and I wonder whether that is why she was able to do it. In some cases of this sad illness, where the patient is only partly conscious of this physical world, perhaps their soul is more free to travel in a spiritual world. There could be a similar explanation for my daughter's wandering: having only recently come to the physical world, and not yet fully a part of it, a baby's soul still has a certain freedom of movement. It's not quite the same thing, but there have also been many recorded cases of living adults' souls appearing in the physical world far from their bodies. These are called 'doppelgängers', although in this phenomenon the soul does not seem to be conscious of their own activity. Whatever the explanation, it was rather lovely that this lady wanted to spend time with and show her love to her family.

All these visitors were coming with love but, because they were not always being acknowledged, they had become a pain at times by moving objects around and making noises. I sat down for a coffee and a conversation with the daughter, helping her to understand her own abilities and reassuring her that there was nothing to be afraid of. She could even ask them all to go! I also showed her how to put herself in a bubble of protection and warned her that, when her baby arrived, it was likely to attract a whole coachload of spirit tourists coming to say hello. She would need to know how to move them on if they were a nuisance of any kind.

Back to the space clearing, the main house had an overwhelming feeling of anger and hostility. This was due to the spirit of an old man, Juan, who had been a violent, angry man and a mean wife-beater who had controlled and bullied his way through life. He didn't like the fact that he was dead and so had lost his control. He was really not a nice man and that energy was everywhere. The owner had even had dreams of a man with his hands around her throat.

I cleared all the energy and moved on the spirits, paying special attention to Juan. No-one wants someone like that it their home. Then I programmed the house to be happy, loving and abundant. The strange noises in the middle of the night then stopped and my client reported that everything seemed much calmer.

A villa that I was called to also had a nasty piece of work hanging about, with a similar case of soul travel. The owner had space cleared the property before and had done a good job. However, there was still a very strong feeling of anger and frustration that she hadn't been able to shift. I soon discovered that this was due to a spirit man, Fred, the father or at least a father figure of the man of the house. Fred was an abuser of the worst kind and controlling, still having a very negative effect.

Interestingly, a much gentler spirit man, Frank – I think he was the owner's grandad – had also come in, trying to calm the energy and smooth over the disturbing situations. Altogether, the energy was like a rollercoaster, as though the owners were stuck in the middle of a battle between good and evil. I cleared away all the negative energy and put a protective bubble around the property so that Frank could still visit but Fred could not. Then I programmed the house to be positive, trusting, open, healthy and happy.

Unfortunately, due to complicated family histories, neither of those names could be confirmed. However, I was confident that Fred was the owner's father, born with that name although he was not known by it. He was a convicted abuser and, again, was still alive but with dementia.

The owner has reported that the home was much calmer after my work and that her husband had even started doing jobs around the house, which he had never done before in all of their many years of marriage!

I find it fascinating that the soul of a living person seems able to visit their family members. The cases I have described both involved dementia and I had another experience of this strange phenomenon when I had a remote space clearing job and was working from a friend's house.

A spirit man came through to me loud and clear, giving me the name John. Because this name had appeared in a lot of the clearings I had been doing, I questioned it and was told very emphatically, "Yes, my name is John."

He had a message for his daughter, that he was sorry he had left them "too soon", at around the age of thirty, and for everything they had been through since. He wanted her to stop crying and remember the good times. He also wanted me to tell her that he had been there every time she was upset, giving her a hug.

Now, the owner of the house I was clearing had no idea what I was talking about. So I started trying to find out who John belonged to. I asked at the circles I hold but, no, he was not for any of them. I was at a loss to know who he was and for whom this important message was meant… until I stayed at my same friend's house again and there was John.

I hadn't even thought he could be for my friend, as her Dad had only died the year before and was a lot older than thirty. But when I asked him if he was connected to her, he told me that he was. So I tentatively told my friend and the astonishing truth emerged: she confirmed that John was indeed her Dad and that he had been ill with dementia since his thirties. It seemed as though he believed he had died then and I guess, in a way, he had.

I had the privilege to do an oracle card reading for my friend's mother later and did wonder whether John would come and say hello. I was delighted when he turned up at the end of the reading to bring a message of love to his wife.

These experiences were truly eye-opening. John had passed to spirit but what he told me was a revelation. He had only died the year before, in his seventies, yet he was apologising for leaving too soon, in his thirties! My friend told me that the dementia had started in his thirties and he had spent the last ten years or so of his life in a care home. John himself, though, had the impression that he had passed to spirit much earlier than his physical body had actually died: he had been separate from his body, as if looking down on the shell left behind.

This has to be one of the most unique, and longest, cases ever recorded of an out-of-body experience (OBE).

What is really interesting is the apparent evidence that the souls of those afflicted by dementia – and perhaps other sad conditions, like coma? – are able to travel to other places and often do so. The soul is not feeling the pain that such illness subjects the loved ones to because they can move in a world that has no time, no walls and no suffering.

I have also described two other cases during my space clearing work of visiting spirit parents who were suffering with dementia yet still still very much alive in their physical bodies. The mother of one client often visits her in Spain, even though her body is in the UK and the dementia has robbed her of memory and the ability to care for herself. This mother had not always had an easy relationship with her daughter but now, in this space between worlds, she comes to look out for her and to bring love. That is a rather beautiful thing.

The other case involved a father who did not come from a place of love but of control. Before his dementia, this man had been an abuser and a convicted criminal, and even between worlds he was up to no good, creating disturbance and the ominous feelings of danger and of being watched. I did my best to block him from going near my client's home and opened a pathway for him to move on, no longer stuck in his old ways of wanting to terrorise people. The home, at least, has since been much calmer.

We should not, I think, naïvely believe that nasty people suddenly repent and become loving when they do pass to the spirit worlds. I can only hope that this man will not continue to be the evil person he was this time around and that he will get help to sort himself out on a soul level. Interestingly, I have found in my work that the spirits who are 'stuck', or earthbound, are usually the ones who were unpleasant in life and do not want to give up control of others, even after death.

My message is this... If you have a loved one living with dementia, and feel that their soul is visiting you, please try to believe that this could be true. Talk to them with love, because their soul can hear you. And please be kind to yourself, too, allowing yourself the time and space to grieve properly, not just when they have passed over but before. Grieve for the person they were and the unrealised life you could have had with them. Yet also be comforted by knowing that, on a soul level, they are free from many of the restraints and sufferings we endure in physical life. It is my hope that these stories of souls being able to travel more freely, at peace and without pain, will be helpful for you.

Incidentally, you may be wondering, as I do, why I keep bumping into spirits named John during my space clearing! I began to notice a pattern and asked my guides, "Really, another John?" The answer that comes back is always "Yes!" So I did some research and discovered that, over the last five hundred years, the most popular names in the UK have been John and Mary. (Oddly, I haven't bumped into any spirit Marys yet!) In that time there have been nearly six million Johns. In Spain, I have also come across the equivalent name Juan frequently, a name that appears consistently in the top twenty of boys' names over that period. The name comes from Hebrew and means 'God is gracious'.

As we have seen, clearing the energy in a home has many benefits, including improving the condition of an illness in the family. My clients come to me for this and many other reasons such as sleep problems, unexplained activity, difficulties with selling their property, legal issues, uncooperative tenants, to increase business or simply to make a house feel like a home. Some clients are just curious to see 'what will come up'.

In my opinion, every home needs to be space cleared (my own home gets cleared regularly) because, even if a property seems perfectly peaceful, any of us can unwittingly bring negative energy into the space with us. I have many clients who return at least once a year, or if there is some kind of disharmony in their world, because they notice a big difference when their property has been space cleared.

Of course, I do not take the credit for the work I do. I am just a channel for the angels and spirit guides to do their stuff, needing a human link to the physical parts, and I just have to trust what comes through. The results, however, speak for themselves.

So, does everyone need to hire someone experienced and professional like me? No, that's not always necessary and I believe that most people could do it themselves. However, this work is not recommended for those who have any kind of mental health issue or may be afraid of what they will discover. Several clients have come to me because they are not confident enough to do it themselves, or the problem seems too overwhelming for them to confront.

Of course, I do have a couple of particular advantages, one being a ready-and-willing team of angels and guides who know how to use me! The other is, to my own surprise, an ability to clear a property remotely from a floor plan. This is especially valuable when we don't have access to the property for some reason.

If you would like to try space clearing for yourself, you may wonder whether you will see spirits and the history of the property. I believe we are all capable of this so you may indeed see things. However, you may not see a thing (if you are nervous you are less likely to receive information) and I do not always even see the history that my clients already know about their properties. On the other hand, sometimes I see everything and more! It all depends on the particular property and the energies and spirits within.

Remember, we are only the channels for higher forces to work through us. Our intention is everything so we must not get hung up on the details of whether we are 'doing it right'. We cannot do it wrongly when we only ever work for the highest good of all and affirm, when we begin, that we are open to the highest and most positive influences. Nothing evil or dangerous can attach itself to us when we take care to protect ourselves spiritually, as described in my first chapter.

The bottom line, though, is that space clearing still works even if we get no hidden information. Magic still happens, as a home is cleansed of negative energy and disturbances, allowing greater peace and harmony and light to take up residence.

I hope you may feel inspired, as I have been, by the following channelled message from my guides.

Space clearing has a profound effect on properties, the occupants and the world in general. At this time of great change on planet Earth, we are working with numerous lightworkers to help more and more people rise up from the slumber they have been trapped in. We, the lightworkers of the hidden realms, want all those who are able and contracted to do so to awaken and to become the persons they were intended to be.

We are here to help. We want you to live in Heaven on Earth. We want the shadow of evil, hatred, envy and greed to move out of your world. You can do this by changing your energy, by being as positive as you can every day. We want you to check in with your higher selves, to listen to the guidance that is coming through and then to act on it. We want you to be happy, healthy and have abundance of every kind in your lives.

Your purpose here at this time is to be happy and to help push through the new reality that is attempting to come through. These are exciting and sometimes terrifying times, but you can do it. You are here right now in this time to remember your own connection to spirit, to the universe and to each other.

The work starts and stops with you. You are more powerful than you can imagine, and we are here by your side every step of the way. Life, your life, is meant to be experienced. You cannot have the light without the dark. Having said that, we want you to shine your light on the darkness and bring through a new age.

If you are reading this then you are being called to shine your light, to be authentically yourself. This is all we need, want and ask. We walk by your side, and we will hold your hand when things are difficult. You are never alone. You are loved. You've got this.

It occurs to me that many people confuse the terms 'ghost' and 'spirit', using them interchangeably as though they are the same thing. That is not really the case.

I'm sure everyone is aware of traditional ghost stories in which a phantom suddenly appears on a lonely road at night or walks silently through the corridors of an old building (clanging chains are pretty rare). There are even astonishing accounts of entire armies appearing on ancient battlefields, apparently still willing to carry on the fight, and of ghostly aircraft still attempting to land on World War II airfields.[4]

These entities are essentially imprints on the Earth's energy fields, in ways that we do not yet understand, of past dramatic or highly emotional events. In my own accounts of space clearing, I have also described sensing the memory of individuals and their experiences attached to properties. These have often been of sadness or fear although, happily, there have also been joyful feelings.

---

[4] *Ghosts of War* by Glynis Amy Allen and Graham Adrian (Local Legend, 2024) has more than two hundred such evidential stories from across the world and throughout history.

These memory imprints could be called 'ghostly'. They are not intelligent and they cannot interact with us.

But there is another kind of ghost, less benign, that is essentially an earthbound spirit. This is often related to a person who has died violently or suddenly, or who has had a traumatic life, or who was a strong character still believing that they have 'unfinished business' or that they are owed something. Such individuals are unable to move on and, indeed, most of them are just not aware that they are dead.

These ghosts invariably have a dark energy. They are unable to reason with us or themselves and are intent on causing problems, perhaps wanting to scare us or get our attention by moving things, making noises or simply disturbing our feelings. For them, it's a matter of control or power. But it is very rare for them to cause any harm.

On the other hand, spirits are not earthbound and have the ability to move between realms. They are the surviving personalities of those who have passed over to the afterlife. They are light energy, often showing up for their loved ones to help them deal with a situation or just to check in, communicating with us in our dreams, in everyday synchronicities, when we sense particular music or perfume, and of course through psychic mediums.

I have used the term 'spirit' throughout this book because I believe we are all energy. Fundamentally, we all have light and dark in us, we are all capable of good and bad because earthly life is one of contrasts. If we believe in reincarnation, then surely we have all been the victim and the perpetrator in past lives. It's just that ghosts have not found a way to let go of the life they led last time around, rejecting any help they may be offered.

But even the worst human being has a spirit that is not inherently evil and is able to move on to the afterlife where, I believe, our souls can assess our past behaviour, learn from the experience with the help of guides and then grow in positive ways.

Perhaps we need to mention demons... These entities could

also show themselves as ghosts although the difference is that a ghost has lived in a human body and a demon has not. Whilst in my experience most ghosts that have not crossed over to the light are not inherently evil, demons certainly are. There is a great deal that, of course, we do not know about the spiritual or alternative worlds, but we do know that evil exists. Think of 'fallen angels'.

Thankfully, real demons are few and far between. My understanding is that they can be harder to 'move on' yet, with our intention for the highest good of all, any ghost, spirit or demon can be helped to find the light. I firmly believe that the light always wins over darkness, and maybe that's one of the reasons I am able to play my part.

My earlier account of meeting 'Gollum' raises the question of 'possession' or spiritual 'attachment'. Again, these are conditions that many people confuse interchangeably. Spiritual attachment, of the kind that I described, is not pleasant but it is much better than possession, although both are fairly rare. They can occur when a person is going through great suffering, physically or psychologically, and their essential energy is low, making them an easy target.

Both cause the victim to behave in uncharacteristic ways that can be upsetting for their loved ones around them. This can manifest in depression and a loss of joy, loss of vitality and hope, psychosis, aggression and violent tendencies, addiction and dependency, sexual perversion and compulsive immoral behaviour. Of course, all of these can have other causes and, sadly, mental health issues are very common nowadays. Occasionally, though, a case may be caused by a dark spirit setting up home in a person.

Possession is when an entity hijacks a person's actual consciousness, taking over their thoughts, whereas attachment is when a spirit piggybacks on someone but remains separate from them. It is not only dark or evil entities that can attach in these ways, but also 'lost souls' who, when their bodies died, were frightened and latched onto the nearest living body to make them feel safe. This is still an unpleasant thing to experience, having a spiritual parasite that feeds off the victim's energy.

Nonetheless, I repeat that such situations are very rare. Moreover, there are easy ways to protect ourselves by vibrating on the highest frequency that we can. We do this by experiencing joy, happiness and fun, and by expressing gratitude for everything we have (even if it isn't everything we want). The benefits of this deliberate approach to life are immense. Not only shall we repel dark spirits, we find more peace and happiness in our lives and therefore attract even more things to be grateful for.

No-one wants a spirit on their back! But the dark doesn't like the light, so let's be the light, shining brightly in everything we do.

8

THE CAVEMAN

Meeting a real caveman was quite a surprise. I'd been asked to investigate a home not far from where I live because the owners were struggling and seriously considering moving. They didn't really believe that I or anyone else could help with their problems. But they'd heard me give a talk on space clearing and had been told by other clients of mine about the transformations they experienced, so decided to give me a chance!

The house didn't feel like home, they said, and there had been one issue after another. First it was the water, then the electricity and finally the Internet. It had cost them thousands of euros to put these things right yet still more problems kept popping up. It was physically dark when it should have been light and airy. The lady of the house had even started dreading going home and would sit outside in the car for a few minutes before entering.

The property was only about an hour away so I decided to do an in-person space clear. As I arrived I couldn't help noticing the stunningly beautiful antique front door, a must-have purchase by the owners. It did, however, bring its own history with it. I picked up that it was from a monastery, a silent order, and there was still the residual energy of a short monk in a brown robe struggling to open it and rolling his eyes every time the wall-mounted bell was rung. In my mind, I was shown that very ornate bell beside the door.

As soon as I entered the property, I understood the darkness my clients had been talking about. The dining room should have been much lighter with the number of windows there, but the energy was so depressing, thick and dark.

Then, all of a sudden, I met him. The spirit caveman was wearing animal skins, probably rabbit. He'd had to fight to survive, was a loner and really didn't like other people as he didn't trust them. He was angry that people had moved onto his land, his home, where he'd lived in a cave below the house. I was shown the original Indalo Man cave painting as representing the time he lived there; later research dated this to 2,500 BCE.

My spirit guides made me laugh, saying that he communicated to them – he had no language as we know it – that he found life much easier now that he didn't have to hunt for food. He lived here because it was near a body of water, which was not visible to me. But he didn't know he was dead and was very confused and upset by people being on his land. The only thing I could pick up about his death was that it was caused by a heavy blow to the skull.

As I moved through the home I came across feelings of sadness in the kitchen that continued onto the terrace and into the spare bedroom and bathroom. It was a feeling of depression and not being able to speak freely, of being controlled. All of this energy was coming from the past owners and the present owners later confirmed that they'd bought the house from a woman who indeed seemed controlled and was clearly depressed.

Thankfully, the lounge not only had the most amazing views but a much more peaceful energy. There were some sharp edges caused by the other disturbance in the house, but generally this was more the energy of the current occupiers. However, the main bedroom was again really dark with heavy energy. After I had sent the caveman away it became much lighter, although the owners did need to use sage in there for a few weeks to stabilise the energy fully.

The original cave was clearly visible from outside but not accessible. So I was surprised to come across, in my mind, another male spirit, much taller than the caveman and dressed in black, cowering in a corner of the cave. I was given the 1920s as the time he had died here. He was a quiet spirit, though, and didn't want to communicate with me.

I clearly felt that the house had never really been lived in, which I put down to the caveman to a large degree. The owners confirmed that it had been a holiday home. The previous owners had not been there for years and it had been on the market for a long time before they bought it.

This house was actually very beautiful but the whole area around it had an uncomfortable feeling. Years ago, the land between the house and the sea had been covered by lakes and the area had also been heavily mined in the late nineteenth century, which may explain the disturbed energy locally.

Well, the owners of the house were overjoyed by the work I did and decided not to move because the place was physically much lighter and now felt like their home. And they are no longer sceptical about space clearing! It is always a privilege to work with angels and guides to make people's lives better.

By contrast, I was later asked to clear an apartment that was only about ten years-old and had only ever been lived in by one family. The problem was that my client's niece, living there, was having trouble at school; something was badly affecting her mental health and her family were really worried about her.

Immediately, I got the sense that the issues were a lot older than the apartments, which didn't make sense to the family. But it was clear that some disturbing residual energy was coming from a building that had once stood on the same plot or on the road nearby. It wasn't easy to pinpoint the exact location.

The apartment indeed had a black cloud of sadness throughout, really heavy with fear and emotional pain and a lot of tears. There were memories of divorce, miscarriage and death. A man had died there of old age, bedridden and very thin and drawn. Juan had had a hard life, working the land, and I also saw a donkey connected to him somehow. This was all residual energy, though, and he wasn't there now.

However, there was one spirit who was often there and this was the owner's grandmother, Rosalin. She had a round face that was always smiling even when things were hard, which they often were. She wanted the family to know that she loved them and was proud of them all. She also wanted her granddaughter to talk to her.

My client was able to confirm that her grandmother was indeed around, as her sister had seen her. I suggested that if she felt it was appropriate and not scary, my client could reassure her niece that she was safe and never alone. Her great-grandmother and spirit guides were there to help. Then I programmed the apartment to be happy, healthy and full of love and laughter, helping the niece to do well at school, have good friends and feel safe and confident. I recommended placing a small rose quartz in the laundry room as this area was an unusual shape that needed extra help.

My client later informed me that things had totally changed for her niece. She was now doing well at school, she had made friends and all the problems she'd been having had gone away.

Isn't it fascinating that energy from long before a property existed can still have such a profound effect on it and its occupants? This family were aware, yet secretive, about their ability to connect with the spirits of their ancestors, and were open-minded enough to come to me on the quiet for help. The niece must also be naturally sensitive to energy, otherwise she would not have been so affected by it.

With young teenagers having problems at school, I would not normally think that space clearing could resolve all their issues. Yet, for this receptive young girl, it made all the difference. Even after all the years and properties I have space cleared, the results still sometimes surprise and delight me. Being a teenager is hard enough without the added stress of negative energy at home.

The owner of a different, much older apartment was at her wits' end. She wasn't at all sure that I would be able to help even though I had done work for her before, helping to sell a property. This situation was quite different. The property had been fully renovated just before she moved in but, only a few weeks later, there was damp everywhere. Water was running down the walls and black mould was threatening to overcome the whole place. The new laminate floor had lifted so much it had caused a step in the middle of the room and was totally ruined.

Frustratingly, the management company refused even to look at the source of the problem, claiming that it was due to an outside drainpipe. The insurance company refused to pay out and the previous owner was taking no responsibility, despite not having declared the issue.

Understandably, the situation was causing no end of stress and upset. Quite apart from the inconvenience of it all, the owner was worried that the black mould would cause health problems for her and her young son.

The overall energy there was of sadness and loneliness. I got the year 1924 as when the property was built but the layout had been dramatically changed, from the original one-bedroom to a small three-bedroom apartment. There was a residual memory of an old couple in rocking chairs in front of the fire. The lady had outlived her husband and would wear a black shawl, sitting staring at the empty chair where he used to sit. A very sad yet somehow also heartwarming thing to witness.

The area had changed a lot since the Twenties. Back then it had been a poor area with several minority groups and gypsies, not a safe place to be and often targeted by the Guardia Civil. They discriminated against anyone who lived there, no matter who they were, what their background or how old they were. These apartments had been home mainly to old people and had seen a lot of suffering, sadness and loneliness.

Now, surely, you may think, what we had here was a physical problem and nothing to do with 'spiritual energy'? Well...

everything is energy and we are all connected by it! I cleared the flat on a Sunday and at lunchtime the very next day I received a phone call from a very excited client.

"Oh my God, space clearing really works!"

That morning, the insurance company had agreed to pay out. The previous owner had suddenly taken responsibility for withholding information and agreed to pay towards the costs. The management company had also already booked for someone to come and look at the pipework. In less than twenty-four hours everything changed in the most amazing way. Of course, the work took some time to be completed, but my client is now over the moon and living happily in her 1920s apartment.

As we have seen, residual or spiritual energy can have disturbing effects on people, especially children. The very young seem especially sensitive to 'other worlds' and a more serious case was brought to my attention by a friend of mine. Her sister had just had her young grandchildren come and live with her and the little boy was struggling. He was constantly angry and, worryingly, was even hurting his little sister.

Something had to be done. The family were already receiving other forms of psychological support but, as spiritually aware people, they were throwing everything at the problem both traditional and metaphysical. So could space clearing help?

Straight away, the first and strongest image I received was of a little spirit boy call Tom. He was about four years-old, the same age as the grandson. He showed himself to me crying with a fever and pain, and he kept telling me that he wanted to "go home". This led me to believe that he had just been visiting when he got sick and then passed over. This had been in the 1980s. I also got the feeling that this had been his grandparents' house – another connection to the little boy who was living there now.

Unintentionally, of course, he was having a negative impact on everyone in the house, bringing feelings of sadness and depression. Everything felt like an uphill battle for them, nothing was straightforward. I believe the occupants had even heard him crying at night, which would definitely be unsettling for the children. I was able to move him to the light.

This house had suffered quite major bomb damage in the past and had needed to be partly rebuilt. There was indeed a bunker in the garden which thankfully had saved the family as no-one was in the house at the time of the bombing. The residual energy of those terrifying days was still present, though, which would have been causing the feeling of not being entirely safe.

One other thing that came up for me was much more pleasant: young women dressed in 1940s clothes and uniforms. (Later, I researched what I saw and it would appear that the uniforms were of the Air Corps.) The women were dancing and singing around an old radio set and having a really great time. I left that imprinted memory alone, to help bring fun, laughter and music into the home.

For such a young spirit, Tom had been having a huge effect on this property and the family living in it. The owner told me she could feel that I had done the clearing before she was actually told it was done, and she definitely noticed a positive change as soon as she came home. Most importantly, although her grandson still has issues, he is much calmer and has stopped "shouting at invisible beings" (Tom). At least, the energy in the house will now support him and not add to his problems.

Do you believe that the spirits of the dead hang around in the graveyards where they're buried? After all, why would they want to do that when there is a lighter, happier afterlife world for them to move on to? Surely souls would want to be near their family or a place they had loved… unless they don't know they are dead or have 'unfinished business'. But then it isn't going to be a graveyard they're stuck in. Nevertheless, many people say that they feel a dark and disturbing energy in such places.

It was another first for me when a client for whom I had space cleared a number of properties asked me to investigate her sister's home because she couldn't settle there and was having a hard time. The house was opposite a cemetery and my client suggested that perhaps some of the energy coming from there was affecting the house. She provided me with plans of the cemetery as well as of the house.

There was mainly negative residual energy in the house itself. This was connected to the village clearances that had happened in the area in the late eighteenth and early nineteenth centuries. The tenants on the land were forced out, often violently, by wealthy land owners. I confirmed this later by research and also discovered that there had been settlements here all the way back to the Bronze Age.

The pain and distress of people being thrown out of their homes while close to starvation anyway was bringing a sense of turmoil, desperation and panic to the modern house, whose occupants must have been feeling unsettled and having problems sleeping. It was a busy, rushing and chaotic type of energy.

A spirit man popped in to visit from time to time. I got the name Fred and the best way I can describe him was like a Toby jug, larger than life, jolly and always laughing. However, in life the laughter had been a cover for the pain he was going through, both mentally and physically. He had very kind eyes, hazel-green in colour and he brought a lighter-hearted mood with him. Sometimes he brought a woman with him too, Edina, who was a softer, feminine Toby jug.

Behind the house was a park area which had a dark energy. My client is a spiritual woman who told me that she often protected her properties and those of family members with 'bubbles of light'. The last time she had done this here, she saw a strange darkness hanging over the place which I am sure was coming from the park area.

I saw a lot of drug activity there, as well as a murder that had happened around ten years before when a blonde woman in her mid-twenties met with a violent death. Her spirit wasn't still there and I couldn't be sure whether the murder took place in the park or in one of the nearby houses, but the energy of the event had stayed and was hanging over the whole area.

The first three spirits I came across were young men, brothers, in what I believe were Air Force uniforms. I was given the name Chris for one of them and surname Burns for all three. They showed themselves to me linked arm in arm, and they also showed me the Bomber Command memorial in London so it's likely that they had been part of that force.

Later, I researched this property more than I normally do after a space clearing because I really wanted to find out more about the cemetery and the spirits I had met. Unfortunately I wasn't able to find confirmation of the Burns brothers but I did discover that a section of the nearby land had been used as a military cemetery.

There was also a little girl in spirit. Around three years-old and wearing a pink dress, her blonde hair in bunches, telling me her name was Sarah. She was happy enough, even though she was looking for her Mummy.

Far less happy was a tall, dark, shadowy male who was very threatening. He would make any visitors to the cemetery feel uncomfortable as his energy was evil. He was connected to the area by work, but this was no worthwhile and legal work – he'd been a grave robber. Such unscrupulous people operated all over the UK in the 17th, 18th and 19th centuries. They would dig up newly buried bodies and sell them, often to medical schools for dissection or anatomy lectures.

In the main, the energy of the cemetery was residual and relating to all the grief the land had witnessed. Much of this was due, as described, to the historic violent village clearances. But equally it's not very surprising that even a modern cemetery should be an unsettling place. It is such an emotionally charged time when we say goodbye to loved ones and it makes sense that we will be imprinting our own pain on the area where we are grieving.

This property had been hugely affected by the entire surrounding area, which was having a negative impact. I cleared the home, the park and the cemetery and moved the spirits I'd met to the light to enable them to continue their souls' journeys. My client reported back that her sister was now feeling much better in herself and was more positive and productive after my work.

This work sometimes brings me into contact with some deeply unpleasant people who are still alive in this world and affecting – or should that be infecting? – everyone around them as well as their property. I was very glad to be able to clear one particular apartment remotely. The owner told me that this place had been occupied by certain family members for many years but it was now time, due to their age and illness, for them to move into residential care because they couldn't cope.

The energy in the apartment was indeed dark and heavy, and the property was filled with confusion, anger, violence and a sense of danger. The tenants seemed to have a feeling of entitlement – they felt the world owed them something, yet they had no self-respect or indeed respect for their home. The apartment was dirty and unloved and I could see piles of papers and other stuff strewn about everywhere.

I could see the man living there. He was big, very unhealthy and unstable and decidedly evil. He had many secrets. Everything that came out of his mouth was a lie although he seemed quite unaware, or simply didn't care, that he was lying. I picked up that there were many more victims of his past behaviour than anyone knew about, or would ever know. Thankfully, by this time he was incapable of bullying or abusing anyone.

My client was able to confirm that the flat was dirty, unloved and full of all kinds of discarded objects. She also told me that this man had spent many years in prison for child abuse and it was believed that there were more victims, unidentified as yet.

I cleared the energy and asked for light to be brought into the apartment and that the occupants should move out for the greatest good of all. As it happened, they didn't leave together as the owner had intended because the man died shortly after the clearing, his wife moving to a care home alone.

9

HOUSES THAT DON'T SELL

I have had the privilege of working with some amazing and, let's be honest, open-minded estate agents both in the UK and in Spain. Space clearing is not something that is widely known about. These agents are willing to go the extra mile to help their clients and, the more they work with me, the more they trust that what I do actually makes a difference. This also allows me to work with properties that I may not have had a chance to do otherwise.

Strictly speaking, because I work for the highest good of all, we do not always need permission from the vendor. Some people certainly do understand the benefit of changing the energy of their property, whereas others may find it too 'alternative'. But the estate agents know best which properties need a helping hand so they send me those.

Sometimes they contact me because the energy of a place just feels somehow out of balance to them. But often they're concerned about properties that have been on the market for quite a while yet are getting little or no interest from buyers. My work invariable brings the desired results. Some properties may still take a little longer to sell than others, even after clearing, if they are niche or remote. But they will sell.

As I have described, sometimes I get huge amounts of information when I work and at other times hardly any. I just have to trust that maybe I don't need to know everything; on the other hand, I am nosy so I like it better when I see lots! I also enjoy hearing back from my clients confirming whatever information has come up and telling me what has happened since.

My biggest problem is when a house is wildly overpriced because space clearing isn't going to solve the problem. Even so, I have seen many such situations resolve. But if the expected results are not forthcoming, I always revisit a property and repeat my work.

This was the case with one particular home where, I was told, the biggest issue was the price holding things back rather than the energy. Having said that, this property was certainly also in need of clearing, not least because the owners were going through a messy divorce and the energy there was very heavy with sadness and historic violence.

Throughout a long period of time this house had been witness to a huge amount of violence (although not by the current owners). In the 1920s it had been shared by four different groups of people living together in it. One of them, an angry man named Bill, had not left. I was shown him as a slight man wearing a flat cap, some sort of gangster who looked like he'd stepped out of *Peaky Blinders*. He'd rented the front room and had died violently, either in the house or just outside. Bill was bringing a lot of anger and aggression into the property and that alone would not have been helping the owners' marriage.

There was also an energy imprint from around the same sort of time of two children who had died from a disease, and I was told that this was yellow fever. Now, I had heard of this but didn't really know what it was. When I researched it later I learned that it is a virus spread to people by the bite of an infected mosquito, with symptoms ranging from a fever with aches and pains to severe liver disease with bleeding and yellowing skin (jaundice).

This seemed quite possible in this case as the house was situated close to some docks. I certainly picked up the energy of docks and dock workers, and it felt like the house had been built by a merchant or someone whose business involved shipping. It was a very strong and definite connection. So these children may have been exposed to the mosquito while working at the docks, or it could have been brought into the house on the clothing of another person who lived there.

The second floor had been smaller in the past and had the residual energy of a servant girl, Rosy, from around the 1890s. She had a beautiful smile and was really young, about 14 years-old. She worked hard but was not treated well at all and she just wanted to go home. Rosy did manage to escape the house because she definitely did not die there, so I hope she had a happier later life.

The property was restored to being a family home in the 1940s and it was actually a lovely house, but it had never been a happy place, sadness was everywhere. Once all the negative energy had gone and I had programmed it to be positive, happy, healthy and abundant for the new owners, it should make a wonderful family home. I also asked spirit to guide the current owners in finding a positive solution to their situation, for the highest good of the whole family.

When the price of an expensive property is reduced but it still doesn't sell, there has to be a deeper issue with it. The agent I was working with had been instructed by the owner of one particular house because it had been on the market with a number of other different agents for a long time. Yet they told her that they couldn't understand why it hadn't sold even after they reduced the price to below the going rate for that type of property in that area. My agent was sure that it needed space clearing and that the owner could receive more for it than it was currently on the market for.

There was a definite and overwhelming feeling of sadness with this one. I kept being shown the horrible brown sofa that had been in my own childhood home, although I wasn't sure why... perhaps it was an association in my mind with the 1980s, the colour representing a sense of depression. There was certainly a spirit couple from that period here. I saw the woman very clearly, with permed hair and blue eye shadow, though I couldn't make out the man's features. This woman came with feelings of despair, sadness and emotional pain, along with being unable to get out of bed.

I also picked up the energy of a child who had been kidnapped and the house felt like it was stuck in the past, somehow still connected to that event. There was the awful feeling of not knowing which way to turn, of total confusion... and the name Jane.

I cleared all the energy, moved the spirits to the light and programmed the property. The agent, who had fantastic local knowledge better than the Internet, confirmed that there had indeed been a child kidnapped and murdered in the road. Well, within two weeks the house then had twenty-two viewings and numerous offers, and the sale proceeded fast. The owner was over the moon after such a long time with no interest.

I have said that some estate agents are very open-minded. How often would you expect one to say, "You need to clear this flat for me, it still has the deceased previous owner living there..."? The situation was not helped by the fact that every time the vendor, who was the spirit lady's daughter, went in she would say hello to her Mum!

Again, this property had been on the market for quite a while with other agents. It was in a retirement complex so was a bit more specialised than other flats. However, it should have been getting more interest than it was because the energy of the place was really lovely.

The agent was correct, the old lady was very present indeed. She wasn't 'stuck', she was just worried about leaving her daughter and had been following her around, looking after her as she grieved. And actually she was also enjoying the flat more than when she'd been alive because now she was free of pain and could move around freely!

I received the name June but I don't think this was the old lady. Sometimes retirement properties can be affected by the illness and death coming from other nearby homes, although there was little negative neighbourhood energy affecting this place. Just to make sure, I put a protective spiritual bubble around the flat so that energy from the other flats could not disturb its lovely feeling of calm and peace.

Finally, I suggested to the old lady that it was time to move on, to start the next part of her soul's journey, but she wasn't quite ready to leave her daughter yet. She did accept that she had to 'let go' but said she would still pop in to see her daughter from time to time, to bring her love. Viewings then started to come in quickly for this lovely home.

This was a very telling situation with a lesson for all of us. The loss of a beloved family member, friend or pet can be truly heartbreaking and it is natural that we should grieve for them. We who remain in this world need such healing. However, extreme sorrow can sometimes prevent our loved ones from continuing their own healing journey in the afterlife. An inability to accept their passing can keep them tied to us and their familiar places. Alternatively, as in the story above, our loved ones may be unwilling to move on because they are trying to comfort and reassure us. It's a very delicate balance that we all need to come to terms with.

We see in many of my accounts that the residual energy of spirits can have a major impact on the residents of a property as well as its sale. This is so even when the spirits are not connected to the present owners and, indeed, may have lived many years before.

The overall energy of one particular two-up, two-down terrace house was definitely wobbly. It had started life in the early twentieth century. The owners at that time were not rich people and had worked night and day to pay for it. They loved it, it was their pride and joy. I was then told that some twenty years later it had been rented out to what felt like more than one family. It had the feeling of bedsits about it.

The first spirit I came across was Sarah, who was in her late teens or early twenties. Sarah was hiding in the loft space, where

I saw her cowering in a corner trying to escape from her husband. I was told that this was the 1930s, that he was a lot older than her and that she had basically been sold to him by her family. He was a violent man and she had died at his hand, her body hidden either in the house or very close by. Unsurprisingly, the energy she brought to the house was fear, loneliness and mistrust. I felt that the current owners must have been experiencing trust issues since living there.

As it happens, the spirit of her husband, Robert, was also still there. He was a weasely little man with a dark and very uncomfortable presence about him. The owners may well have seen shadows of him or felt him nearby, because he liked to hold onto doors, especially of the loft, so people felt they were locked in. He thought it was funny.

I also picked up the energy of two young children around three and four years-old, who had lived there not that long ago. They were terrified of the loft because Robert had held onto the door and they had been stuck inside it.

I asked that all these spirits be helped to move to the light and programmed the house to sell. The agent then told me that, before space clearing, she had struggled even to get into the property with the keys because it felt as though someone was holding the door closed. You really cannot make this stuff up! The property soon had a number of viewings and the sale went through.

I often work with an estate agent in Marbella, who calls me whenever there is a troublesome property. Sometimes, she herself can feel that the energy is disturbed and that something is preventing the property from moving. The first flat I cleared for her had been stuck on the market for no apparent reason.

This flat had a heavy feeling of sadness about it which turned out to have an unusual source. I soon picked up the energy imprint, not the spirit, of an older man, Peter. He had been very ill with a long-term condition like emphysema, coughing and with trouble breathing; he was on oxygen and spent a lot of time in bed. He was holding onto life – and the flat – although he was still alive and in a care home or hospital.

Moreover, it turned out that Peter was not even the owner of the flat! No-one seemed to know who he was, and he was definitely not attached to the land or the villa that had been there before the flats were built. It's possible that he had been a neighbour whose energy had spread to this property, which can happen. Whoever Peter was, he was bringing frustration with him because he felt stuck and that's what he caused for the flat. After I had cleared his energy from the property, it soon sold.

Encouraged by this success, the agent and I developed a great business relationship and the next property I cleared for her was on a golf resort. This one also had a unique issue, despite the overall energy of the apartment being very calm and positive. Actually, that was the problem! The tenant had developed very strong cords attaching her to the property because this was the first place she had ever felt safe, her life before having been one of trauma, abuse and uncertainty.

I cut the cords between her and the apartment, as well as those of any past occupants, and programmed it so that she would feel safe to move on. She needed to do so for her own wellbeing. But the flat did not sell.

Now, I have my own professional standards, quite apart from my developing relationship with the estate agent, so I revisited. To my amazement, the energy had totally changed. It was almost as though the tenants were wearing concrete boots to stop themselves being moved because they no longer felt safe.

I soon discovered that the main cause of the feeling of unrest was that they had somehow unknowingly brought a spirit into the flat, who showed herself as a dark, hooded female. She seemed to be attracted to young couples and intent on causing disruption even though she was not linked to them or the apartment. She had just attached herself to them from somewhere else. This is very rare and I had only seen it happen once before.

The attachment was now causing arguments and the tenants were also getting headaches. I sent the spirit to the light and cut all the cords and attachments again, asking for the concrete boots to be removed! Thankfully, the apartment then sold.

Another property in the same complex had a very strange energy with it. A particular issue was that the owner needed to sell yet, at the same time, didn't want to because she had tenants in it and couldn't afford for the place to be empty before it sold. Once again, then, there were cords to cut.

But there was something else. When I checked into the energy, I saw a black, heart-shaped hole over the apartment. I could not understand this but the agent could. It turns out that a young woman had been abducted while living there and had never been found even some ten years later. My client was convinced that although she had not gone missing from the apartment itself, this was the cause of the energy hole I was seeing. I did get the sense that the young lady was no longer alive, and I just hope her body is found soon so that her family can grieve properly.

I cleared the energy and filled in the heart-shaped hole, also cutting the cords that were causing the owner to hang on so tightly. The flat did then sell, a bit slower than I would have liked as there were complications with the tenants, but it was still a good result.

My friendly agent then asked for my help with a property where the simple problem was the eccentric owner herself. There wasn't much of significance to report except that the energy was rather dark and heavy, due to the owner being a hoarder. Sadly, hoarding affects – and can in turn be a symptom of – mental or physical ill-health, and this lady was having a hard time.

Clearly, it also doesn't help you with selling your house and the agent told me that she had been working with the owner to clean the place up. Thankfully, it hadn't quite got to the stage where you couldn't enter or move around the house. But the owner was very nervous about everything and, working remotely, I was shown her speaking really fast and coming across as manic. She was just trying to get through each day and hide how scared she was.

I also picked up that there were cats. One really made itself known to me. He was a large, dark grey cat, good-natured and still in a physical body, wanting my attention. The agent confirmed that the animal was indeed very demanding.

There was also the residual energy of an older-looking Spanish lady from the 1980s. I think she was only around sixty years-old but hadn't worn well, her appearance not helped by the black dress she wore to show that she was in mourning. She was round and short, her eyes full of loneliness and sadness.

I programmed the property to empower the owner, helping her to clear out some of the clutter and, most importantly, for her to feel safe and calm. It still took a long time to sell, though.

Some properties are slower to sell than others even when the energy is squeaky clean. Naturally, if it is very remote, as many are in the area where this agent works, it is likely to take longer – as it will if it is overpriced. Sometimes it just takes time for the prices to go up in that area and then the property will sell. There are many factors in this business and one has to be realistic, yet space clearing does always have a very positive effect on properties and their occupants.

We came across one particularly unforeseen factor when the agent, who is very sensitive to energies, asked me to clear a certain property because she'd been shocked at how fast it had become a negative place to be. The house was owned by a Reiki Master healer and had been full of positivity when the agent put it on her books. But on her second visit to do a viewing it felt uncomfortable and dark.

It transpired that the owner had invited another 'spiritual' person into her home, but that person did not have the wellbeing of others in mind and had been negatively affecting many other lightworkers in the area. (A lightworker is someone who does spiritual work for the greatest good of all, such as by healing of any kind, giving clairvoyant or oracle card readings, or even space clearing!)

The situation here was nothing less than a spiritual attack, which is when a person or an entity energetically hurts someone else. Such an attack is not physical, but the victim may well feel physical pain, depression or anger. I really don't know why a so-called spiritual person would want to hurt another; to my mind they are not on a spiritual path however much they may like to believe they are. If they are not working for the highest good of all, as far as I am concerned they are working with evil, which we already have too much of in our world. The only mitigating factor I can think of is that a person like this might have started out with good intentions but has developed mental ill-health and lost their way.

Now, in fact I didn't know about the spiritual attacks before I started clearing the house. But its energy was really bad, uncomfortable and unstable and I felt physically sick. There was also a strange and very unpleasant smell, almost indescribable, and I kept hearing the phrase 'sick to the stomach'. It was like something very negative and violent had happened there. There was also a black shadow that moved very fast.

I removed all entities and negativity and programmed the house as always but unfortunately the negativity continued. The agent then told me her thoughts about the spiritual attack, which I think explained the dark shadow, an energy form that the new resident had brought in. She described the situation to the owner, who of course understood energy but found herself unable to disconnect from the attacker even though we all now knew who it was. We can only guess at the owner's motivations.

This is an unusually ethical agent who is not afraid to tell the truth and will not take on properties unless she knows she can sell them. She found herself left with no other choice than to walk away and take the property off her books.

That hardly seemed fair, yet life often isn't. We all need to accept that there are some things we can do nothing about. Sadly, though, there seem to be many people who like to think of themselves as victims of life, which keeps them stuck in a dark place and unable to move on. This was the case with another property that the agent asked me to clear. She had just been instructed, although the house had been on the market for a number of years.

The main energy of this house was of hardship, anger and 'life just isn't fair!' The property wasn't in its original form, having been totally rebuilt, but there had been a dwelling there since the 1920s. The negative energy was coming from the original home, around the areas that were now the main bedroom and lounge. I sensed explosive anger, as though everyone needed to walk on eggshells; one minute all was fine and then… bang! There was a feeling of needing to be in personal control and to control others.

Then I saw him, a spirit man who was trying to hide from me. He had been seen out of the corner of the eye in the form of a dark shadow moving quickly around the house. He was the original occupant. In death he was as he had been in life, quiet but with a simmering anger about him, believing himself to be a victim of unfairness. That's why he hadn't moved on. He didn't want to let go of his anger and the 'poor me' attitude, even now that he had the opportunity of a better life in spirit.

I cleared all the energy and helped to move this troubled soul on. The agent was delighted by the results and within days she had viewings and an offer. The buyers had to deal with some personal matters but once they were resolved the sale went through.

10

DOWN TO BUSINESS

When a business is being run from a home, there can be added complications. In particular, the energy and layout of the various spaces need to be considered carefully. And whilst there may not be disruptive 'spiritual guests' around, the influence of other characters involved in the business will inevitably be affecting the owner's personal life.

I was called in by one particular gentleman because, although his property had been space cleared by someone else in person about ten years earlier, he felt it needed to be done again because his business was somehow not moving forward as he felt it should. I worked using a detailed plan and soon discovered that he was right.

The energy was completely stagnant, which explained why his business was stuck. I sensed that he was actually considering moving, although for now I encouraged him to enjoy the house until it was the right time to move on, living in the moment and appreciating everything he had.

I got the powerful smell of menthol, which a little odd, perhaps a medication used by older relatives for relieving congestion or aches and pains. Certainly, both the owner's mother and mother-in-law in spirit were popping in from time to time to give their love and see how the family was doing. He would know that they were about as he could also smell their perfumes, or a song would play on the radio that reminded him of them.

The main issue in this case was something that most people never give a thought to, the layout of rooms and their furniture. The important home office was a small room and the desk faced a wall with the owner's back to the door whenever he worked. This is really bad from an energy viewpoint because it represents turning your back on clients and not welcoming them into your business. So I strongly suggest that anyone who runs a business should move their work desk so that they can see the door, helping to attract more clients. This may sound a bit weird, but it really works!

In this property, however, because of the size of the office there was no way the desk could face the door. To solve the problem, I suggested that he hung a mirror above his desk so that he could see the door. Energetically, this would be a sign that he was 'open for business' and ready to receive customers, even via the Internet. I also suggested clearing out a cupboard on the landing, as there was something in it that had negative memories attached to it. Because of its situation in the property, the cupboard also needed a crystal within it to help cleanse the energy.

My intuition told me that there were a few specific warnings for my client. The first was that he should trust his own feelings about the people he worked with – if something didn't seem right, then they weren't the right people. Secondly, he needed to be reminded that it was perfectly okay to want more abundance! This message is indeed for everyone reading this account. Our abundance supports the world so we must all aim high. We deserve abundance in all its forms.

A third message is also relevant for everyone, that we need to try and achieve a good work/home balance. Hustling to create a business is not always the best use of one's time; people are much more productive, and create a better flow of energy towards them, when they take time for themselves.

In no time at all the owner of the property contacted me to say that he had just had the best business meeting ever. He had put up the mirror and placed the crystals I recommended. He had ditched an untrustworthy business partner. Significantly, he had followed his own intuition and was changing direction, taking his business back to how he had originally envisioned it, much more heart-centred.

The use of a mirror and crystals in this account are examples of *Feng Shui*, an ancient art that originated in China. The name translates as 'wind and water', the practice derived from a poem about human life being connected to, and flowing with, the environment around it. Indeed, many if not all ancient cultures had their own similar rituals, myths and traditions as past civilisations understood the importance of the energy of the places we live and sleep in. The reason for *Feng Shui* regaining popularity over the last thirty or so years is that it works.

By making simple changes to our homes we can improve the energy flow. We should start by making sure that all hallways and entrances are clear of clutter – it's amazing what a difference this one thing will make to the energy of our homes. In my work, I am often guided to recommend that crystals, decorative mobiles, mirrors or maps be placed in certain locations within a property, to reinforce the energy of a home or business.

I use the same techniques in my own home too. For example, the entrance of my house has a photograph of my family facing the door, telling the universe who lives here and bringing in more abundance. Naturally, I have my desk facing the door of my office so that I can attract clients to my business. This works even for an online business.

Feng Shui is a complex yet remarkably helpful practice and I recommend everyone to do their research and see whether a few simple and comfortable changes to the home or place of work can be made. Without doubt, the single most important thing we should all do to help change the energy of our property is physically cleaning and decluttering it.

Have a good look around at all your possessions and ask yourself: do you love it, do you use it, do you wear it? For example, if we haven't used or worn an item of clothing for a couple of years and we don't love it for a special personal reason, we should get rid of it. What's the point of keeping clothes that are too big or too small just in case we can fit into them again one day? There's nothing worse than wishing we were a size smaller than we are, as it doesn't help us feel attractive and positive. And by giving clothes that no longer fit to a charity shop, not only are we helping that charity and other people in need, but we are also making energetic space for new things to come to us. This makes us feel lighter.

This can seem like a daunting task so we should take small steps and allow ourselves to clear one space at a time. If we only have an hour free, then we must make sure we can deal with the space we want to declutter, cleaning and restoring it in that time. It will not help us feel good if we pull everything out of the wardrobe and haven't got time to put things back. What about that drawer in the kitchen that everything gets shoved into, to be dealt with later? Most of us have one! Even by just clearing that one small space we will feel lighter and better motivated to declutter some more.

Decluttering is not easy in our material world and it takes some determination to let go of things that are no longer of use, broken or don't fit. Yet when we do, and we overcome our tendency to hold onto stuff because we 'may need it in the future', or it was a thoughtful but unwanted gift, it frees us. It makes space for new things, new opportunities and abundance to enter our lives.

All of this is not saying that we should get rid of everything that serves no purpose. Clutter is very different from things that we love. For example, I have several antiques in my home, some inherited and others bought, and their sole purpose is to bring me joy. So they stay.

One particular property had been empty for a long time before the new occupant took it over to develop it into their new office space. She had the foresight to recognise that the place probably needed to be space cleared first. It didn't take long to confirm that she was right.

There was the energy of a short, round Spanish man, Juan, from around the early nineteen sixties. He'd had a great deal of pain in his head, a build-up of pressure, which caused his death; I sensed it was a brain tumour or a bleed on the brain and that he had struggled to function because of it, suffering a slow and painful demise. The general underlying energy of the office space was of anger, despair and failure. I saw lots of books and papers but it was unclear to me what the property had been used for.

However, I did see an old map of the area on a wall and I was told that if my client placed a similar one there it would help the business to be successful. She didn't have one, but after a few weeks the perfect map did indeed turn up. I also suggested that she purchased two citrine crystals to place in the second room, a store or office, where the wall was an unusual shape. I cleared all the energy and programmed the office to be positive, productive and abundant, for all her clients to be a pleasure to work with and for her to have more than enough products to sell.

Since then, the new business has continued to go from strength to strength with new opportunities for expansion appearing on a weekly basis. The reputation of my client and the services she offers grew at an amazing rate and, within less than a year, she already had a very successful and profitable business.

Commercial properties are one thing but I had never been asked to space clear industrial spaces before one owner was recommended to me by a friend because he desperately needed help. His business had lost a few large clients and was on a downward spiral. To investigate the problem fully, we agreed that the best thing to do would be to space clear both his industrial properties and his own house. We also booked in an oracle card reading to focus on the business.

Before I had even drawn a plan of the plant I sensed a problem with the office staff, so I recommended doing staff reviews. Interestingly, my client then told me that he had just started doing reviews that very day. So we were already on the same page.

As I continued to work with the plan, I came across a spirit man called Tom who showed himself to me wearing white boots, overalls and a hairnet. He had died about five years earlier from a heart attack but was unaware that he was dead and kept turning up for work. He wasn't causing any trouble as he was as quiet and unassuming in death as he had been in life, but I moved him on.

However, the overall energy of the whole plant was of sadness and being unmotivated. I received the message that it would be good to play music, to lift the staff's and the building's energy. Actually, my client said they had played the local radio in the past but for some reason this had stopped. My suggestion was to play a station that didn't have news bulletins as, far from helping, this may in fact hinder the energy. Let's face it, the news is hardly ever good, and it sparks a negative or worried emotion in us when we hear it even in the background. My research found that the best music to increase productivity is classical or instrumental.

The energy of the second plant was positive and productive. There had been a disruptive member of staff who had created some negativity but he had left now. I cleaned all that up. My client was a man who valued his staff and tried everything he could to ensure they were happy, but he acknowledged that he'd been forced to let a certain worker go earlier in the year. He did not enjoy sacking people. Indeed, the staff now at this site were happy, content and productive so I encouraged him to keep leading them as he was. They felt valued and would go the extra mile for him and his business.

I continued to work with this businessman on a monthly basis and we were both glad I did when he ran into some unexpected problems. He'd had to take some time off for health reasons and when he returned he was horrified to find that, in his words, "while the boss was away, the children played up." Suddenly, things had changed and not in a good way.

We decided that I would concentrate on the main plant for a few months until the situation was resolved. When you have a building with many people working in it, you have all their energies coming into the area and affecting it. When I revisited the place, what I found was not surprising. The energy was unstable and it felt like being on one of those moving platforms in a funfair. There was also a dark cloud hanging over the place, making all the energy feel even heavier. For my client, this was very disappointing and extremely stressful.

Five staff members were leaving or had already left, and I was told very clearly that there were going to be one or two more people going yet. On the other hand, I was also told that, even though all this was difficult, the owner would be 'clearing out the weeds' and building a really strong foundation. As I worked, an eagle was soaring over my house, a sign that this business was going to soar to heights that my client had not even imagined.

At the same time, though, I was told to warn him to be very aware of his intuition when interviewing new staff and not to hire anyone who may look good on paper but somehow didn't feel right, even if he could not put his finger on why. He needed to trust the feeling and not hire them just because the role needed to be filled quickly, but to slow down and take his time. The right people would be on their way and they would help to take the business to the next level and beyond. Beneath the surface, everything was happening to sky rocket his business.

He was being called to be patient, to trust and not to worry. The oracle card I pulled for him was Archangel Michael, the perfect card for him as I always work with Archangel Michael while space clearing. He is the archangel of protection and helps us to feel safe even when things are challenging. The message was that my client was safe and the business was safe. So he needed to surrender his concerns – not an easy thing to do – and roll with the punches, allowing the miracles in. This was going to be a really exciting phase for his business, although it certainly didn't feel like that at the time when he was up to his neck in difficulties.

It was a true privilege to work with this kind-hearted businessman and I reassured him that the angels were clearing the path for him. His prayers had been heard and answered. He just needed to take a step back for a short time to allow himself to see things clearly and to make space for miracles.

He reported back to me that he was indeed in the process of removing another staff member. He had interviewed a replacement who on paper seemed perfect but hadn't 'felt right' so he had not hired him. It had been a short but painful period that had to be gone through for the business to rise to yet another level.

When I turned my attention to space clearing his home, I found that it was easily the loveliest, calmest house I had ever worked on. Normally people have their homes space cleared because there is some sort of issue to be resolved or because they are intrigued to find out its history. This time, what I found was a really lovely home with great energy. It was full of love and happiness, fantastic to witness. We were just clearing the property to make sure we had covered every base.

The only issue I discovered was a degree of sadness due to grief. The owner confirmed that the family had been through a lot of losses, so this was not a big surprise to him, and even the grief did not distract from the energy of love and peace. I did just suggest placing a rose quartz crystal in the hallway to enhance these feelings in their home, and I removed the slight negative energy of grief. Finally, I programmed the property to be healthy, happy and abundant and, also, for the business to thrive.

I continue to work with this businessman on a regular basis, space clearing his business premises and doing business enhancement oracle card readings for him. We did not space clear the calm house because it just didn't need it. This client went on to acquire two new plants and his business took off. I know things are going to be wonderful, not just for him but for his family and all his employees.

Another client approached me because they had taken over a business that over the past ten years or so had been rented and run by a huge number of different people, not always successfully. I picked up that originally this bar had been a house, and around

1958 someone had opened the house to paying customers, though not as a formal bar. Then it was empty for about twenty years until it was renovated at the end of the last century and became what it is now. My client later confirmed all this history.

Whilst the overall energy was good, there was a strong feeling of jealousy and greed coming from the landlord. The bathroom area was rather odd, dating back to when the property had been a house, and the ladies toilet made me feel sick due to an energy of crying, heartache and pain. This area had once been a bedroom. The house was very basic, built around 1901, and was typical of the houses of that period. The tenants of that time had a lot of struggles and hardship, earning their livelihood by working the land. The upstairs area, which is still unoccupied, had been used to dry meats and vegetables and had never been lived in.

I removed the historical pain and all the stagnant and angry energy that was a result of the place being closed for several years. In the course of my work, I met a spirit gentleman, Pepe, who often visits and wants the bar to do well. He told me he would keep visiting. There was also another regular who had passed away a few years ago and now pops in from time to time. He brings a warm and welcoming feeling, as does Pepe, which is perhaps why customers like this bar.

Finally, I programmed the bar to be happy and abundant, for the customers always to feel welcome and comfortable so they stay and spend their money, and for it to be a place of fun without drama. The business is now doing brilliantly well, and all the staff openly talk to Pepe!

A far less happy situation was presented to me by a lady who had been attacked at her business premises. She had not even been able to enter the shop since the attack, and the energy of that event needed to be removed.

I didn't receive a lot of information. There was a definite feeling of sadness and disappointment, of dreams not being fulfilled, but that had come from the previous owners. Then I was surprised to be shown the image of pigs screaming. It seems that the building had been a pig shed at some point in the past, which is more than likely in that area of Spain and given the building's construction. The pain and fear of those times was still lingering.

Moving on to recent events, I picked up the traumatic feeling of being trapped and backed into a corner. The offender undoubtedly had serious mental health problems, something like schizophrenia, and needed professional help.

I was able to clear all the negative energy in the property and finish by surrounding it in a bubble of spiritual protection that would only allow good to enter. My client then felt able to return to the shop and said, "I can't believe how well space clearing works!" One of her staff also contacted me privately to say she could feel a real difference in the building and her boss was much calmer and more motivated.

I love being able to have such a positive impact for people.

11

INHERITING SPIRITS

On more than a few occasions I have been called on to help people who have inherited properties. The problems involved in such a situation can be complex, ranging from legal red tape or probate issues to disagreements among family members. Then there are the emotional attachments that individuals may have to the property. Sometimes people strongly feel that they should not sell at all because it was their parents' home, even if they know perfectly well that they will never live in the property themselves. Thankfully I have been able to help some grieving families to work through these difficulties and to sell their inherited properties.

I met one particular client when I was giving a talk about space clearing at El Palacete. He was a Reiki Master, so well aware of how energy works, and he just happened to be staying at the hotel on the day of the talk. Moreover, he was very excited to find out what space clearing was, especially as he really needed some help.

He had two properties that he had inherited and needed to sell. Both of them were priced well and neither he nor his estate agent could understand why they seemed to be stuck on the market. The first flat I investigated was very dated yet still a lovely and desirable place.

The energy there, however, was really heavy, full of despair.

I came across a spirit woman named Encarna. She was short, dressed in black with grey hair in a bun, and she'd had trouble breathing. There was so much sorrow, pain and tears attached to her that made me feel very emotional. She was giving the whole property a feeling of sadness and of being lost.

But then I also came across a spirit man, tall with a long black coat. He was a man of few words and didn't want to say anything to me. He was making people feel uncomfortable, as though they were being watched, which they were! He was as creepy in spirit as he had been in life.

The second flat was not as dated and I received the phrase "clean and tidy" and the name Diego. This was a very positive place, filled with love and laughter. Yet as I was clearing this property I was shown why neither of the flats had sold. The owner's father in spirit was holding onto them and I even saw him literally shouting, "I worked hard for this, I'm not leaving."

My client confirmed that this was indeed likely to be the case. His father had worked very hard and never wanted to sell any assets. I picked up no other information, so I moved the spirits to the light, cleared the energy and cut all the connections to the previous owners that were preventing the flats selling. Finally, I programmed them to sell quickly and well and for both my client and the next owners to be healthy, happy and abundant. Much of the information I had given my client was confirmed, and I was delighted when he told me soon afterwards that both the properties had sold.

Apart from the influence of Encarna and the creepy man, the biggest problem for these properties was the energetic cords attached to them. These are like umbilical cords that tie people or properties to other people, situations or memories. We all have such energy cords that attach us to places and to one another. For example, think about your parents: no matter what kind of relationship you have with them, there will always be an energetic cord of attachment to them.

And when a departed spirit has a strong cord of attachment

to a property, it can literally hold it back from selling. It doesn't matter how much the new owner wants to sell, how cheap it is or how good the agent is. If those cords are thick enough it just will not sell.

In the case just described, the attached energy was extremely negative. But it can also happen that the previous owners of a property had very happy and positive experiences there, which can be difficult to let go of. So when I cut cords, it's the ones that are having a negative impact on the property or preventing it from being passed to new owners.

Inheritance can cause no end of disputes in families! Sometimes there is no Will or it is unclear. Sometimes the departed's final wishes can come as a big surprise to their beneficiaries – and all the more so to those who expected to be beneficiaries but find themselves excluded… One client came to me because of just such legal issues that he hoped I could clear. He had inherited a property but another family member believed strongly that this was unfair and was causing no end of problems.

There were no spirits lingering in the corners of the property, but all the residual energy there showed me that this had never been a happy home. The previous occupants had undoubtedly loved their family but struggled to express that love; my client confirmed that this was the case, it had not been an easy place in which to grow up.

This was clearly a place associated with a great deal of manual labour and almost Victorian working-class values. Life here was all about hard work and fun was not something the house had seen a lot of. Just doing the right thing was important, no matter how difficult it was.

I sensed a large man who came with dizziness that made him unsteady, and a stomach problem that was possibly due to a tumour. It made me feel sick. There was also the energy of a small, slim woman, and I got the name Mags. She washed everything by hand and used an old mangle in the back yard. There had been alcohol addiction present too, though not aggression.

The details were confirmed by my client although unfortunately we couldn't find out why I also picked up the feeling of mourning and grief that seemed to be connected to a war grave or a memorial of some sort.

Interestingly, it would seem that the negative energies of this house had somehow been affecting the other family member who had been causing difficulties. After the clearing, all the legal issues were resolved and the property was successfully sold.

It is very rewarding when people return to me with more properties to space clear. I must be doing something right! One time, a previous client was selling two plots of land, the first in Tenerife and the second in Mallorca, so clearly I needed to work remotely. Each case proved completely unique and surprising to me.

After a conversation with my client, it was soon obvious that the first plot of land had some hidden problem holding it back. It was not the only land for sale in the area, but it was the best situated and well-priced. Inexplicably, however, other plots of land were selling and this one wasn't.

As you may expect, this being a piece of land after all with no buildings on it, there was not a lot of information coming through for me at first. But as soon as I started clearing the land, I got quite a shock. I had never seen anything like this before. There was what I can only describe as an American caravan, like the wagons we see in the old Western films. There were people, animals and old-fashioned carts, some with canvas roofs.

The land appeared to have been a route to and from other places, and I kept being told that hundreds of immigrants had walked these trails. This information seemed very odd to me. I knew next to nothing about Tenerife, but surely on a reasonably small island this couldn't be the case? Still, I always trust that the information I am given is correct, no matter how strange it seems to me, so I persevered.

Next, I got the year 1883, which I think was the year that the family had originally purchased the land. These ancestors had intended to build their family home on it and pass it down to their children, but I was told that there had never been any buildings here. The land had never become the original vision that it was intended to be.

The reason it hadn't sold was that there were very strong energetic cords of attachment to the owners. And as the land had passed down the generations, the more embedded the disappointment and regret had become, only strengthening those cords.

My client then confirmed that, yes, there would indeed have been people travelling across the land in caravans and that all through the generations the family had planned to build a home on the land. But these plans had never come to pass for a number of different reasons. The attachment made sense. After I had cleared the energies, the land sold very quickly and for a price my client was happy with.

There were much more serious and sinister underlying problems with the land and property in Mallorca, and my client was having many problems with it. There were paperwork issues and it was just not selling, even though it was well-priced.

The situation here was complicated to say the least. My client had not inherited the property, and indeed he had never even wanted to buy it. He only did so to keep his then wife happy! It was bought from a millionaire who had invested in the site but had gone bankrupt. My client's then mother-in-law had supposedly been renting from the millionaire but had refused to pay the rent, making the man's situation even more desperate.

My client was a good and well-meaning man who had then bought it with the understanding that his mother-in-law would pay him the rent, which of course she never did. To make the situation even worse, a parcel of the land could not be purchased at the same time because it belonged to the millionaire's brother, and he couldn't be pinned down and persuaded to sell.

When I started to investigate the property, the first thing I was told was that my client had bought it because he was the one person who would be able to heal the land. What did that mean? I had never come across anything like this before. Yet as soon as I drew up the plans, the information came flooding in.

This time, the essential issue lay in the very land itself. There was an energy vortex just below the house that had been bringing up evil and darkness, attracting those types of people and conflicts to it since the beginning of time. This vortex brought pain, suffering, greed and jealousy. The worst characteristics of humanity were being attracted to this place.

A building had been there before the present *finca*, a traditional farmhouse, and that building was a place of worship and a space to practise black magic. It had been full of symbols of darkness, both inside and on the walls, and at least one of those walls still made up part of the *finca*.

There was more, even worse. Between 1890–1910, my guides told me, people on the island had been disappearing and this is where they ended up. They had been locked in a cellar, later to become victims of ritual sacrifice. There were at least five bodies on the land. And a really evil spirit named Juan was still there… He was a priest, but that was just a cover for his devil worship.

The energy of this place was so dark that it would turn anyone who lived or spent any time there into something bad, changing their behaviour, causing depression and even suicide. This was a deeply unhealthy place to be. It had caused greed in the man who built the property, leading to him losing everything. The darkness caused problems for everyone, including the previous owner's brother and my client's ex-wife and her mother: he confirmed that both their personalities changed significantly when they lived at the property. They became greedy and depressed and would do and say things that hurt others.

As you may appreciate, this was a highly emotional clearing task for me as the energy was shockingly strong. I had to leave my office a few times to be able to deal with it. I psychically created a huge and impenetrable metal lid to close the vortex and then bolted another cover over it. I moved on Juan and the five souls whose bodies were buried in the garden. I cleared all the energy and cut the ties to the evil history.

This was a very complicated plot, with many different issues going on at the same time. Because of this, I have since returned to clearing it multiple times, and every time I do so I have removed another layer. My client tells me that things are now moving forward legally and the estate agent has received considerable interest.

After this space clearing, I researched missing people for the period 1890-1910 and devil worship on Mallorca. Perhaps unsurprisingly, given the extreme secrecy, there were no results for missing people. However, there is certainly a history of devil worship dating back over two hundred years and some of the fiestas on the island are even still closely connected with the traditions of black magic. I bet the many millions of tourists who flock to Mallorca on holiday would never guess that there were such sinister underlying traditions on the island.

The same client has since purchased two rental properties on mainland Spain and has asked me to clear them before any tenants move in. It is always lovely when people show that they appreciate what I do, and I trust these properties will be less challenging.

I was asked to return to one property that I had space cleared in the past, this time in order to programme it for sale. The only way I can describe its energy now was "wobbly". I sensed sadness and mixed feelings about selling.

There had been a resident spirit called Maria on the previous occasion. At that time, she had been earthbound and was very unhappy that the house had been split up. Indeed, it had a unique set-up. Some of the rooms belonged to the property next door and this house had no access to them. But it also had a blocked off room that no-one had access to. This was what had really been upsetting Maria.

I had moved her to the light on that occasion, yet here she was again. This time, however, she was no longer stuck or causing problems and was free to travel wherever she wanted to, in this realm or another. Her character seemed to have totally changed and now she wanted to help my client. She told me that she would not go to the light "until Juan passes on"; then she would go and, until that point, she would help the owner to sell the house. Well, the name Juan is very popular in Spain and this could have been any one of around two hundred men in this village!

With my estate agent background, I did feel that the agent in this case was not doing as much as possible to sell this property and I passed my thoughts on to my client. The agent could work harder on his behalf by, for example, advertising more widely, getting feedback on viewings and giving weekly reports, all providing reassurance that the agent was doing their best.

But the owner also confirmed that the family had mixed feeling about selling the property, their holiday home of around twenty years. They had made some great memories in it and some of the loved ones they had spent time with there were no longer with them. This was another complication.

As always, I cleared the energy of this unique village house and programmed it to sell, becoming a wonderful home for the right buyer. I was sure that Maria would do her best too, but there was nothing I could do about Juan…

Another spirit, though, was actively preventing a property from selling. The estate agent approached me because she could not understand why it had also been on the market with other agents and was getting no interest. Could I discover the reason?

In fact, the overall energy was good with only a few things that needed attention. One of these was a feeling of grief that was very new; the owners had lost someone close to them not long before and were still having difficulty dealing with it.

But the most troublesome energy was that of a young spirit lady, Laura, in her early twenties. I got the date 1910. She was attached to the land more than the house itself. I saw her in a dirty white dress, running through the area and looking over her shoulder as though being chased.

I also saw what looked like a workhouse. The agent later confirmed there had been a workhouse nearby and part of the building was now being used as offices for the local hospital. It was indeed in view of the street this house was on.

Laura was searching for her son and she showed him to me aged around three and wearing a flat cap. But she was not limited to this property and was searching for him through all the other properties on the street. She was causing a feeling of something missing, something not quite right, a piece of the puzzle not being there. Laura was the main thing holding this house back from selling because somehow she was more attached to this property than the others. The angels helped her to move to the light where, I am sure, she would be reunited with her son.

Part of my work is giving oracle card readings and one lady whom I had read for in the past contacted me again because she had been going through a particularly difficult time with family issues and a very hectic work schedule. The overall energy of her home, she said, was also "bumpy". Indeed, there was no huge surprise there – just a feeling of meeting oneself coming back. Busy, busy, busy.

When I had read for this client before, we had encountered a soldier named Fred and now he reappeared, showing himself in a World War I uniform. He had some kind of family connection, maybe her maternal grandfather or a great uncle. Fred wasn't ready to move on and only had good intentions, so I didn't interfere; he was there to watch over her and was trying to comfort her, wanting her to feel safe. He gave the property a feeling of security and was available for her to talk to whenever she felt low or lonely.

On the other hand, the upstairs of the property, that was

hardly ever used, had a lingering dark shadow spirit. He brought in a feeling of always being watched. This was a very old spirit who'd lived here when the house was new and it seemed to me that he was on watch from an upstairs opening. It would not have been a window at that time as upstairs would have been more open and used to dry food then. My client regularly used candles and sage downstairs and this had kept him at bay upstairs.

The town where this property was situated had a rich history, like many in this area of Spain, and might possibly even had had an escape tunnel at some point on the ground floor like those described in an earlier chapter. But my client's home was situated on the second and third floors with a shop beneath them for which I had no plan, so I was unable to be certain about a tunnel.

Despite such history of struggles, hard work, a lack of time, food and money, the house had always been a happy home and this feeling still shone through. I just needed to clear the turbulent energy of events that had occurred in my client's life over the past few months. Then I asked the angels and guides to take the old spirit man to the light and I programmed the home to be calm, happy and abundant. My client confirmed she felt much calmer now and was able to relax, even with her hectic job.

After clearing this property I was asked by a relative of my client to investigate their home. Who should I come across but Fred again! It turned out that Fred was in fact my client's grandfather who had died before she was born. He is still happily watching over the ones he loves.

It's not always just homes that are inherited and one particular request proved a unique and interesting one for me. I had worked for this client before and was intrigued when they asked me to space clear a vehicle for the first time. I knew it had to be possible, because if properties can retain energy then it stands to reason that so can vehicles.

The van had been inherited from a family member who had not long passed; this person had been a troubled soul and that was very clear to see when I began my work. My client wanted to be able to use the vehicle without the potential danger of causing themselves or others any problems.

I didn't draw the van as I normally would a property plan, because my drawing skills are not up to that; I can use a ruler and draw rooms, but a van is a bit different! So I used a picture.

The energy hit me straight away. Although no spirits turned up, this space was filled with sadness and it felt like my chest was being physically crushed. There was also a lot of anger at not being able to control the sadness and pain. The previous owner had suffered from severe depression, which had led to alcoholism.

My client later confirmed that the van had been owned by someone who had suffered in these ways. Depression and alcoholism are terrible illnesses that can have a devastating impact not only on the sufferers themselves but all their loved ones too.

I cleared all the negative energy and surrounded the van in a protective bubble of light, so that anyone driving it would be safe and protected, with no ill effect from the vehicle's past.

12

UNWANTED VISITORS

Everything fell into place for my eldest daughter to leave home. Her best friend was sharing a flat with three others and when my daughter met one of the flatmates there was an instant spark between them… he soon became her boyfriend. However, he then changed jobs and moved to a different city, not far away, leaving his room empty; but his contract wasn't up for another few months so he would have to keep paying rent. They devised a plan: she would live there rent-free until she got a job. This was all perfect for them both since he was still closer to her than if she had continued to live at home.

Naturally, one of the first things she did was ask me to space clear the flat! This was a genuine request, though, as she is very sensitive and was aware of some activity and a feeling that she, and indeed her best friend, found uncomfortable.

When I started working, I came across a strong and heavy energy of sadness and anger. No wonder it felt uncomfortable. There was a spirit man who showed himself as dark and shadowy, in his thirties. He had lived in the flat in the 1960s and had hung himself. He didn't really want to die and was crying out for attention and love; and now he was angry that no-one found him in time.

I was getting the name John but it was unclear why as the name didn't seem attached to the spirit man and it was not the landlord's name. Perhaps this was a memory of someone else who had lived there. In any case, the energy of the flat was heavy with argument and it had not been a happy place to live. I cleared all the residual energy and helped the spirit man to move on.

But then a few months later more problems arose. This time doors were unlocking themselves and a spirit had been felt in the hallways and in the room of one of the girls. Of course, I made time to clear the place again straight away and was quite upset when I found the reason for it all.

Two of my daughter's flatmates had been playing with a Ouija board, with no real understanding of what they were doing. In fact, they were creating a real problem. First, I came across the spirit of a different male, an older man, one of the girls' grandads. He was not dangerous at all and was not earthbound so I let him be.

But next there were dark and dangerous energies lingering in the hallway, lining up outside the flat and trying to get in. It was difficult for them because of my first space clearing, and if one did manage to enter it was soon forced out. I strengthened the protection around the flat to block them completely from entering. I also gave my daughter a supply of sage and showed her once again how to protect her own energy and how to get any entities to move on.

This will be a recurring problem, though, if her flatmates play around with things they do not understand and cannot control. Everyone has free will, so all my daughter can do is protect her own energy and keep moving anything untoward on, until her flatmates decide to stop. I suspect I shall be clearing this flat on a regular basis.

A Ouija board displays the letters of the alphabet and the numbers one to nine, usually together with the words 'yes' and 'no'. Each person present puts a finger on a small piece of wood called a planchette (or sometimes on an upturned glass), which moves around the board spelling out messages in response to questions asked. There are records of such boards being used during the Song Dynasty in China, around 1100 CE, as a religious practice known as *fuji*.

The modern Ouija board became popular among American spiritualists in the 1880s and was developed commercially by Charles Kennard, the founder of Kennard Novelty Company, who claimed to have invented it with his business partner, Elijah Bond. Originally intended as a parlour game, it was promoted by Bond's sister-in-law, the medium Helen Peters Nosworthy, as a means of contacting the spirits of the dead. It was she who asked the board to name itself, which it did, its next message reading that the word Ouija meant 'Good Luck'.

Personally, spirits get in contact with me directly or through my guides, and my own opinion is that Ouija boards are dangerous, opening up access to energies that we really do not want to be coming into our lives or our properties. Having said that, I do know someone who works with an 'angel Ouija board', helping her to communicate with the angels. As with all spiritual work, if we have experience and understanding of other worlds and our intention is for the highest good of all, we can block any evil or harmful entities.

But big problems arise when people do not have this understanding or do not have proper respect for other dimensions, entities or spirits. This practice is not entertainment. That is disrespectful. Angels and entities of the light will not come to us just to play around. On the other hand, malevolent entities are always looking for any opening they can find to our world, to cause chaos and harm.

I strongly recommend that before anyone engages in any sort of activity that 'calls in' spirits, they check in with themselves. Listen to the intuition's answer. Is it really safe? Communicating and working with spirits is not a game and should be treated with respect. For vulnerable or very sensitive people it can also be extremely dangerous and lead to mental or physical health issues, even personality changes.

A case in point occurred when a lady whose home I had cleared some time before approached me to check on the flat her daughter was living in while at university. The girl had been having problems sleeping and was struggling to concentrate on her studies. I saw that the property was definitely not helping as the energy was heavy with confusion and violence.

Then, when I moved around the floor plan of the small flat, a terrifying scene played out in front of me as a previous female tenant was violently attacked. She was confused as to why she had been targeted and was petrified, being dragged from one room to the next. I heard the sound of screaming and the fear of death was in the air. Thankfully, I was able to see that the victim survived the attack, although she had been injured.

Still, this energetic imprint was most definitely impacting the sleep and emotional wellbeing of my client's daughter. Things improved for her after my work and she was able to concentrate on her studies once more. But then a couple of months later her mother contacted me again because her daughter was having more problems. This time I was shown that she had inadvertently brought a dark spirit home with her.

How could this happen? Well, university life can be a wonderful experience and a time of self-discovery, but there are also risks. Maybe this girl been playing with a Ouija board, trying to call up spirits, or been with other people doing something similar. Sometimes things like this can happen when a young person is feeling a bit low and finds themselves in the wrong place at the wrong time, in the company of thoughtless people where a lot of alcohol is consumed or drugs are being used.

This story ended happily, though, as after the second clearing and removal of the spirit the girl did so well with her course that she was offered her dream job, even before her exam results were out. Of course, space clearing cannot guarantee your perfect job or great exam results, but it definitely will not hurt!

One of the reasons for our energy getting low and making us susceptible to spirits of a negative kind is the influence of a human 'energy vampire'. Usually, such a person will have no idea what they are doing and are not deliberately wanting to harm others, although occasionally it can indeed be intentional. Have you ever walked away from meeting someone and felt totally drained, or confused and in a dark mood? The chances are that you were in the presence of an energy vampire.

These people tend to be very negative, they want to tell you all the bad news about all the people who have died and how the world is a mess and we are all doomed. They will often see themselves as victims of injustices and a stream of things that have gone wrong in their lives. What they never see is that they are actually helping to create the worse possible outcomes, because that is what they are expecting to happen, and they spread that way of thinking to others, almost literally draining their energy.

Now, we all have the power to control our own thoughts, our reactions to other people's behaviour and life's situations, and this in turns creates the world we see. Many people therefore choose to no longer turn on the TV news because it's rarely positive and we can feel our energy go down as we watch it. Similarly, there seems to be no end of doom and gloom on social media. But we can choose to scroll past this and focus instead on positive quotes and posts about people achieving their dreams. This makes us feel good and lifts our energy. The more positive our thoughts and the things we say, watch and read, the more positive things we will see in our lives.

Energy vampires try to suck all of that from us. We can feel our energy leaving us and going to them, like a jug emptying into their glass. That's why they will want to be near us, they want our energy; they will feel amazing every time they interact with us, leaving us feeling negative, hopeless and just plain exhausted.

The good news is that learning how to protect our own energy can really help. This way, we are blocking others from stealing it and putting ourselves in a much safer place, far less likely to attract unwelcome spirit energy too. Regular meditation can also help us stay at a higher frequency, enabling us to attract the things we want and deserve into our lives.[5]

Apart from the influence of other people, there can be powerful energies in the very ground beneath our feet. I was once asked to space clear a renovated barn. My client didn't have any particular issues but was intrigued to see what would come up because he thought the property might be on a ley line. These are believed to form a network of energy paths in the Earth that run in perfectly straight lines with focal points along them, often at holy sites, churches, beacons, sacred wells and burial mounds.

My client was not disappointed. The first thing I heard was counting… one, two, three, four… then marching. There were seven men in World War II uniforms who had stayed here one night on the way to an army camp. I hadn't been to this property and didn't know the area at all, but the owner confirmed that there were a number of army camps locally.

This wasn't the original barn, which had been destroyed by fire in the early 1900s. I sensed a boy of about twelve years-old who had slept in the original barn around that time. The place was filled with straw and there was a black horse, the boy's clothes were rags and he was very skinny due to a bad harvest. He was not related to the owners but was a farmhand who worked in exchange for a bed and food. They were kind to him and this was residual energy, not a spirit. There was one spirit in the barn, that of a little brown dog, a terrier called something like Chip. He was staying there to protect the owner so I left him.

There had been a Roman road on the land here and I felt the imprinted energy of a large army marching past in red uniforms with shiny brass helmets. I was also told there were indeed strong

---

[5] There are a number of meditations on my website, all free and around ten minutes long. https://www.samangelguide.com/blog/categories/meditations

ley lines here, which makes sense because the Romans often used ancient Celtic 'solstice paths of the sun' or other existing tracks to build their roads on.[6]

The Celts were advanced in technology and had a similar system of straight roads in place before the Romans arrived. But they had no tradition of writing, which is why today we have all heard of the straight Roman roads and not those of the Celts. Many believe that they built their original roads where they did to harness the energy of the Earth, thus coinciding with the ley lines.

There was more evidence to back up the theory that this barn was on a site of special energy. The owner told me there had been an old stone chair here, and the local legend was that this was used to tie witches to. In mediaeval times it was commonplace to bury murdered witches or those who had committed suicide at the crossroads of ley lines because these points were believed to have spiritual significance and heighten paranormal activity.

I was also shown a family graveyard, really old and with a metal fence around it. The owner confirmed that it was no longer visible but thought he knew where it was. There was an underground lake and river, too, which supported the theory of ley lines as water courses are often associated with them.

Our modern knowledge of ley lines owes much to the Herefordshire antiquarian, Alfred Watkins, who devoted his life to investigating them.[7] Watkins himself was simply interested in the alignment of ancient sites and didn't interpret them as esoteric. He noted that they also include waterways, naturally formed ridges and various paths the ancients used as trade or migration routes. His work became more well known with the emergence of New Age theories in the 1960s.

Watkins found such lines passing throughout Great Britain.

---

[6] A solstice path of the sun is the line created when the sun hits the Earth at the time of the solstice, either in summer around the 20th of June or in winter around the 21st of December.

[7] *The Old Straight Track,* Alfred Watkins (1925; new ed. by Abacus, 1988)

For example, the St. Michael's line connects dozens of landmarks along a 350-mile stretch between Cornwall and Norfolk. Some believe that this ley line extends all the way from Ireland to Jerusalem and takes in the French Mont St. Michel ley line, which is on the same orientation as Notre Dame cathedral, perhaps even connecting the American Stonehenge in Salem, New Hampshire (infamous for the Salem witch trails), to Stonehenge in the UK.

There are thought to be ley lines all over the world, linking up focal points like the Pyramids, Stonehenge and Machu Picchu. Whilst ancient sites and monuments are some of their markers, their names and how far they run varies depend on which authors we read. There's the Viking line in Scandinavia, King Solomon's in Israel, the Titicaca-Cuzco-Machu Picchu line in South America and the Sedona Vortex line in the USA.

In various ancient traditions, ley lines have been called by other names. There are fairy paths in Ireland and dragon lines in China, whilst the Incas referred to spirit lines and Aborigines speak of dreaming tracks.

There seems to be a particular correlation between ley lines and ancient burial sites. According to researcher and author David Cowan[8] these lines were once called 'faery paths', along which funeral processions passed on their way to a church cemetery. Not all faery paths were straight, though, many being circular. The dead would be placed outside the lines, perhaps to ensure that any negative energy of the body would be neutralised by the Earth's natural forces.

With such a wealth of historical references, it's clear that our ancestors were more spiritually connected than modern people; they were more tuned in to the energy of nature and knew how to use this energy to help others and themselves. Cosmic energies meet the Earth along ley lines creating powerful focal points where sacred rituals were performed.

With humanity and nature so out of harmony, perhaps now is the time more than ever for us to embrace and get to know

[8] *Ley Lines and Earth Energies*, David Cowan (Adventures Unlimited Press, 2003)

ley lines. Throughout this book we have seen many examples of sad or traumatic or violent events leaving their residual imprints on the energy fields of the Earth. In turn, these memories have affected properties built on the land and created disturbances for the people dwelling there.

But the natural life force of the planet also flows right beneath our feet. Standing or walking on or near ley lines can ease ailments and make us feel more alive than ever before, taking away negativity and pain. Their energy can aid spiritual awakening, giving us profound moments of clarity, opening the doors to higher states of consciousness and inspiring creativity. They help us access ancient knowledge from both the Earth and our ancestors, leading us to a deeper understanding of ourselves and the world we live in.

The energies at ley line focal points can be very powerful so sensitive people need to be aware of this and ensure that they protect themselves spiritually (as described in my first chapter). Given this, meditating there can lead to greater insights and heightened experiences, a deeper sense of peace than with meditation elsewhere. This will be enhanced by using crystals since they will be positively affected by the natural energy of the line, protecting us and healing any negativity we are holding onto.

If you feel inspired to investigate the energies of your own property or of nearby places in nature, do first protect yourself and then open your mind to spiritual guidance. You could use the meditations on my website, reach out for angelic support if that feels right for you, and then… see what comes up!

Journalling is a great tool for recording our experiences and keeping track of what is going on in our lives and how we are feeling. Personally, I find it really helps me to stay focused on what I want to achieve on a day to day basis, and also helps me get rid of any negative feelings or thoughts I may have. Then later, it's satisfying to record what has been achieved during the day.

The best thing about your journal is that it is for you and only for you. You don't need to be worried about spelling, grammar or even if everything makes sense at first. You don't need to be concerned about others' beliefs or attitudes.

And it can be done at any time of day that suits you. First thing in the morning with a cup of tea is good as this helps us to get the millions of thoughts out of our heads and enables us to be more productive as we go about our day. Then if we have had interesting experiences during the day, we could record them in the evening so that our minds are calm for sleep. It doesn't matter if we only write a few lines or several pages.

This is our own special book whether it's plain or pretty, simple or decorated, and we can write exactly what we want to without judgement. Some people like to reread what they've written before, to refer back to earlier experiences, but some never do. Whatever we have learned stays within us anyway.

What will you discover about the energy of your own surroundings?

13

A BLESSING OR A CURSE?

People often remark to me that it must be so wonderful to have these special spiritual gifts and, yes, there have been many times when it's been a real blessing. On the other hand, I am only human and I have noticed that my ability to see other worlds does depend on what is going on in my life at the time. I have the same everyday worries as everyone else and when I have been under great stress my psychic senses may not be so clear. It's important that I keep working on myself.

Can you imagine, though, what it's like to be almost living in two (or more) worlds at the same time? When all is well in my life, I can just be visiting somewhere and suddenly get such breathtaking images of times gone by. Of course, with this often come the less pleasant views of dark things that have happened in these locations. There are definitely certain places I will actively avoid or, at least, I know that I need to place myself in a huge fortified bubble before returning there.

The gift can kick in at the most inopportune times. When I first met Barry, who would later become my husband, he took me for dinner at a wonderful old English country pub. I really wanted to focus on the occasion and on him. But as we sat there eating and drinking, I couldn't fully engage with our conversation because there were around twenty spirits dancing near the ceiling. Yes, dancing. And they were showing me the most amazing colours, it was extraordinary to watch. I asked Barry if he could see them and unsurprisingly he said 'No'! So I went on to describe what I could see. Somehow this didn't put him off and at the time of writing we have been together for twenty-five years.

As if that wasn't enough, Barry certainly knew what he was in for when we visited Hampton Court a few years later with our young family. For myself, the experience was fairly 'normal'. As I walked round the kitchens – I had bubbled up, as I was expecting activity – it was packed with kitchen workers from all sorts of time periods. The so-called haunted area, however, had no spirits at all. Then as we moved around the amazing building we came to the throne room and I knew before I entered that there was at least one ghost lingering in there. When the door opened, I could see what I can only describe as a courtier scene playing out in front of me. Then all of a sudden a spirit man came flying towards me which was my cue to leave and go back into the corridor.

I wanted to visit the old apartments of the Court, not because of the exhibition there but because I wanted to see inside the rooms. I took our eldest daughter with me but actually the apartment didn't reveal much and I felt rather disappointed.

Meanwhile, because those rooms were up a lot of stairs and our youngest daughter Mysty was around two and a half years-old and in a pushchair, Barry took her to the maze. He had a much more exciting time. As they entered the maze, he jokingly asked Mysty to direct them to the centre from her pushchair. She took him straight there and then said, "He's not here." He then asked her to get them out and, without one wrong turn, they were at the exit.

The attendant on duty could not believe they had been to the centre and back in such a short time, and said it had never happened before. Hampton Court maze is the oldest surviving hedge maze in the UK and is quite difficult to navigate. Created in around 1690 for William III, it covers a third of an acre and we were told that the average time to get to the centre is twenty minutes. Mysty did it in a fraction of that time.

About ten years later the two of them visited again and Barry asked Mysty to get them to the exit. She did just that with no wrong turns. He complained that they hadn't gone to the centre and Mysty calmly replied, "You asked to go to the exit!"

Is it possible that she had a past life there and that's why she knew her way around? And who was the man she thought should be in the centre? She couldn't say, but because she was always fascinated by Henry VIII – as a young child she would shout out his name whenever she saw pictures of him – I am guessing it was him. Another strange thing is that on both trips a photograph was taken of her. When we came across the two pictures several years later, we realised that they'd been taken in exactly the same place. Hampton Court still has a huge pull for Mysty.

Sometimes our family outings turned out to be less pleasant for me. We used to live close to the Devil's Punchbowl in Hindhead, Surrey, and would often go for walks there. This is a very large natural amphitheatre and a site of Special Scientific Interest, most of it very beautiful and peaceful. One Sunday we were out walking and decided to take a different route to our normal one. This turned out to be a bit of a mistake.

As we rounded a corner, I found myself confronted by the vision of five men all hanging from different trees. This area had been well used by highwaymen in the eighteenth century as it was the main route between London and the naval dockyards of Portsmouth. (The Old Portsmouth Road was later replaced by the A3). It is known that hangings happened here, as a warning to would-be robbers, but I wasn't expecting to travel back in time and see them.

We carried on and came to what looked like, to me, a random bit of concrete. It seemed like a strange location for this but what was even stranger was that I then saw a horrifying pile of bodies and the wreckage of a plane on it. A very disturbing sight on what we'd hoped would be a peaceful walk.

My research later revealed that there had indeed been a plane crash at this site. On 6th May, 1945, thirty wounded US airmen had been on their way home to America when the weather changed and their plane hit a radar antenna. It crashed to the ground and landed on a concrete hut, also killing the person inside.

You will have realised by now that strange things often appear randomly to me, like seeing people at the side of the road who aren't there. Sometimes, as above, this can be quite disturbing. But seeing buildings in their former glory is always a pleasure and I never get bored of seeing ruins as they once had been – and how they could be again. (Maybe that's why we live in a house that's around three hundred years-old.)

Two hotels that I have stayed in really stand out. The first was in the Sierra Nevada where we had gone for a few days on our way to a holiday. It was in really bad shape and because of that it had been cheap to stay there. Barry wasn't overly impressed. But I loved it because I could see all the former glory, the beautiful staircase, the wonderful light fittings and the amazing swimming pool (now green and in complete disrepair). I could see the people in all their finery, too. This had been a private home for some seriously rich and important people. Stepping back in time to experience this was just wonderful, although it was tinged with sadness at what the place had become (and Barry still wasn't impressed).

The second special hotel was in Genoa, Italy. Downstairs had been lovingly restored and the owners had managed to keep the original opulent feeling of the building. Our bedroom, however, had been butchered in the 1970s, complete with an avocado bathroom suite. Yet I could see how this room had looked, with its amazing four-poster bed, rolltop bath and black and white tiles. It had been truly stunning and only the richest people would have been able to stay there.

There are some things of the past, though, that are perhaps better left in the past. The hotel did boast its original early twentieth century elevator. Yes, it was beautiful and had that open grille style. This was fortunate when it broke down with us in it because we were able to get the attention of someone walking up the stairs nearby. It took an hour for the hotel management to get it moving again and free us. We climbed the stairs after that.

In the past, before I fully understood the importance of protecting my energy, and remembered to do it, I would have a strong physical reaction to some of the unpleasant scenes I witnessed and the spirits that lingered there and were attracted to me.

Gibraltar is a case in point, and a place that I am in no hurry to revisit. As we walked through the old city entrance the spiritual activity hit me like a ton of bricks. I was engulfed by spirits who all wanted my attention, and they took my breath away. I had to get out of there fast, the feeling was so intense and uncomfortable. As soon as I got out of the archway area my breathing returned to normal and I was able to put myself in my protective bubble. Given its military history, Gibraltar is full of such activity. Now that I am more experienced, maybe I would be interested in space clearing some of the properties there… or maybe not.

Cathedrals and churches do tend to have a lot of spirit activity going on and they totally fascinate me. But I fell into the same trap when visiting the cathedral in Seville. As soon as I walked in I realised my mistake and quickly protected myself. In every area of the cathedral there were spirit families huddled and I sensed fear and sadness. This seemed strange to me until I learned that in the sixteenth century it was used as a place of refuge from the city officials. These *alguaciles* were not allowed to enter and arrest people there. There are still chains surrounding the cathedral that mark the boundary between the City and the Church.

There has been many a time when I have had to turn around at the door of a shop or pub because I knew I wouldn't be welcome. Of course, when I am working it is a different matter and I don't care whether the spirits, even the malevolent ones, want me there or not since I have an army of angels behind me and always work for the highest good of all. It is a very different story, though, when I am just being me. I can't very well suggest to a shopkeeper that I should space clear their property. I would probably soon get a reputation as 'that crazy woman'!

But it's not just buildings that can be affected by past trauma, sometimes it's the energy of a whole area leaving a real impact on those living there or even just passing through.

One example is the region of France where the Battle of the Somme took place more than a century ago. We were on holiday and as we were driving close by we decided to go and visit a preserved supply trench. I knew we were getting close, not just because of the sheer number of military graveyards but the feeling the area had. It was like a large black cloud still covered the whole area. We drove through villages where there was no-one about and there were no bars or restaurants to be seen. Even though the buildings were modern, they seemed hollow and empty despite being lived in. There seemed to be no birds or any other signs of wildlife.

The sadness and the pain the area had suffered had a huge effect on all of us; it was very emotional and we had to fight back the tears. When we arrived at the trench and the small restaurant that had been created next to it, the atmosphere didn't improve. I could tell that there were spirits about, but they were almost hiding there in the shadows. Talking to the owner, it became clear that the trench had been preserved out of remembrance for those who had lost their lives and out of the owner's sense of duty. Yet even the restaurant had no life and the owner himself seemed to be almost a shadow of a person, stuck in that black cloud of depression, sadness and fear.

I had a similar feeling in a small village in rural Almeria, Spain. At the time, space clearing was a hobby for me and not my business. But I had been speaking to a lady I knew about it and she was very keen for me to come and investigate her home. As I drove into the village it was like the sun had disappeared from this beautiful area of southern Spain and a huge dark cloud had taken its place. The villagers all appeared to be dressed in black and walked with their heads bowed.

When I stepped into the house, everything became clear. I could hear screaming and crying and saw a child being pulled from the house. As I moved on, I was shown that this hadn't been an isolated incident, there had been a reign of terror over the whole village for not complying with the Franco regime. Hiding the children or leaving the village became a terrible choice. But with little money and few opportunities for escape – there weren't many places to run to at that time in Spain – many were not able to leave their rural farming communities.

Those that stayed faced whatever came their way the best they could. The losses were huge and the feeling of that grief, along with frustration, fear and mistrust, is still very much in the air of this otherwise beautiful Spanish village.

Well, I cleared the energy of the house, which would have had some impact on the area around it. Yet in order to remove all that sadness I would have had to clear every house… or would I? I am beginning to formulate an idea about this, not yet put into practice, and only time will tell if it is possible successfully to space clear whole villages.

My experiences in that village were not yet over. At the time, Barry and I had been looking to buy a house and the lady I cleared the property for had arranged for me to view a home that was on the market, just around the corner. I already knew that there was never any chance of us moving to this village, the energy was too draining, but she had arranged it so off I went.

The three-story house was a very dated and I saw the spirit woman as soon as I walked in. She was sitting in a rocking chair in a room that had the stairs going up to the other floors. And she was definitely not happy because she did not want her home to be sold! As we moved through the property so did she, following us through every room and up the stairs.

When we got to the very top, there she was right in front of me. And then it happened: she tried to push me down the stairs. I put my arm up to stop her and grabbed the banister with my other hand. The agent probably thought I was pushing a cobweb away and I decided it was best not to tell her about the spirit woman.

As I mentioned, these were early days and at that time I was not knowingly working with the angels and did not fully understand about protecting myself and my energy. I now know without a shadow of doubt that I am always protected and that no malevolent spirit can get close to me.

Another very disturbing trip, when I was not doing the spiritual work I do now, was to a small commune in Italy called Calcata in the Lazio region, about fifty kilometres north of Rome. It is a very strange place, balancing on top of a hill, and is certainly an ancient settlement. The Santissimo Nome di Gesù church dates back to the fourteenth century.

I was really keen to visit because I had read that the original town had been abandoned in the 1930s as it was thought to be unsafe due to parts of the volcanic mountain falling away. Then in the 1960s a group of bohemian artists and hippies moved in and began restoring the historic centre of the town. There are now something like a hundred people living there as an artistic community and it is a visitor attraction, with artisan shops and restaurants.

But it is fair to say I couldn't get out of there fast enough. Even as we walked towards the place I started to feel very uneasy.

In the last chapter I discussed the belief that the very Earth has a primaeval energy or life-force flowing through it. As well as certain places, or focal points, being associated with magic and mysticism, others have attracted people with darker interests, intent on harnessing the natural energy for personal power and control.

Most of the houses in Calcata also have deep underground cellars and some believe that many of these are in fact tombs. Most of the houses looked uncared for and unloved, which didn't help the uneasy feeling I was getting. Without making any comment about the modern community, I got the definite sense that the town had borne witness to dark arts and that some very sinister things had happened there in the past.

I was unwilling to hang around to see what would come up. What I believe without any doubt in my mind is that ritual sacrifices and some form of devil worship had taken place there.

We have seen that properties and the land itself retain energies of the past, but what about physical objects? This idea is exploited by directors of horror films, in which ancient artefacts or even toys such as dolls carry some kind of paranormal and usually scary force. It certainly stands to reason that some pieces of jewellery in particular would hold the energy of their owners, given the strong emotions often attached to them. This is why some mediums use personal objects to connect with the souls of the departed. 'Reading' an object like this is called psychometry.

I have only once tried to read jewellery and to be fair it didn't go very well, probably because I was drinking coffee and not taking it seriously enough; I hadn't aligned my energy to be in the right place to receive information.

When I space clear, however, I am totally in the zone and I once worked on a bed in a second-hand shop. When I visited the shop the owners commented that they were surprised the bed wasn't selling. The energy coming from it was certainly unsettling, so I spoke to the owners who agreed that I could clear it for them. I don't normally suggest space clearing for people randomly because that would be interfering in their lives, but I did know these people well. And although they didn't fully believe in the energy of things, they were opened-minded enough to allow me to go ahead.

The energy of the bed was emotional and made me want to cry. What I saw was a young woman tied to it while in childbirth. It was a traumatic scene in front of me that explained why the energy was so sad and disturbing. I cleared the bed and programmed it to sell. The whole area felt much better then, but there was another piece that was bringing a feeling of anger with it. It was a large dresser and the information I received was about addiction and desperation. I cleared that too and the whole shop felt lighter.

Interestingly, soon after my visit the shop suffered a water leak. This did not seem like a coincidence because water, in spiritual terms, represents the cleansing and purifying of energy, literally washing the negative away. In the following weeks, sales increased for the shop.

If you have pets you might have noticed that animals are very sensitive to the paranormal and more aware of spirit activity than we humans. Perhaps this is because they haven't, like most people, been 'programmed' by society that it isn't acceptable to pay attention to other worlds, or it may simply be that their senses are more finely tuned to energy vibrating at a higher level.

We have a spirit cat who often likes to visit our home. Both my girls and I became aware of him and independently we all came up with the same name for him, Blu. Now, our living cat Charlie is normally very laid back, liking nothing more than food and cuddles. But when Blu visits all hell breaks loose, with Charlie going totally wild, jumping off furniture and running around the house like a mad thing. This can last a minute or an hour, depending on how mischievous Blu is feeling that day.

So if you notice that your pet seems to be aware of something that you can't see, acting strangely or staring at a particular spot, you may have a spirit visitor. And if your pet is clearly frightened, you may need a space clearer!

ADDENDUM

I hope you will indulge me if I include here a few testimonials from clients, so you don't just have to take my word for it that space clearing really works!

Nicola, England
I had an ongoing issue with a property and didn't know which way to turn. Sam had helped me years ago and I called upon her help again to carry out a virtual space clearing (providing the necessary information, as no walk through of the property was possible). Just a little over twenty-four hours from when the space clearing had happened, I gained information, clarification and action which I can now carry forward. Sam is wonderful and the service she provides amazing. Thank you so much.

John, England
I was introduced to Sam through a friend and what a great experience I have had. I had a life path reading and space clearing at my home and business premises. Sam was so accurate with what she was saying and one of the topics I had only discussed that morning with my management team. I have already started to see and feel a positive difference. I would highly recommend you try Sam's services.

Rafa, Spain
A fantastic experience with the sale of two energetically stagnant homes. Highly recommended.

Frank, Spain
I had my house space cleared by Sam and the change in the household after, for the better, was amazing. She was very professional and insightful.

I would highly recommend her.

Howard, Spain
Sam offered to space clear my house in the UK as it was just not selling. I did the house plan as she requested and she did her stuff. I could not believe what she then told me! What was the fire in the back bedroom? And who was the angry man living in the house? She appeared to know all about it. Within a few days the house had sold.

This woman never ceases to amaze me. I would recommend her and her spirit circle and personal readings wholeheartedly. Incredible!

Kerry, Spain
Sam space cleared my house via a floor plan. What she discovered was amazingly interesting, and gave an insight into lives lived at my home in the past. I would highly recommend Sam.

Trudy, Spain
I have had many readings from Sam which have all been amazing and very positive and calming. Two weeks ago, I asked Sam to space clear my house as it had been up for sale for a long time with no luck. Sam space cleared the house, gave it good energy and within a week the property sold!

Shaun, England

Hi everyone. I just felt that I had to write something here and say thanks to Sam.

Although to a large degree I never felt like anything was wrong or missing in my life, I had been told on a couple of occasions, in quite inexplicable circumstances, that something was 'blocking' certain elements in my business life.

I am an advocate of the power of energy so, when Sam contacted me out of the blue and at a critical time in one of my business ventures (a couple of days before the launch of a new opportunity), I felt overwhelmingly that I had to listen. More than that, I had to take action.

I followed Sam's instructions, even though we're over a thousand miles apart, and waited for her report on how she had cleared the house. The report came far quicker than expected (the next day) and the last sentence was, 'When you notice the shift, please let me know.'

That shift also came quicker than expected. Without going into detail, my own physical and mental state subtly changed for the better almost immediately.

I had the most incredibly positive telephone call that same afternoon with my business partner. And my launch event a couple of days later was an amazing success and the future is looking bright.

Interestingly, a colleague at the event, a lady who had mentioned 'blocks' to me a year ago, commented on how she could see a change in me and wasn't in the least surprised when I told her what I'd done.

In short, because I've gone on a bit here, I can't thank Sam enough for what, to me, has been a massive shift in my personal energy – like a weight that I hadn't even realised was there has been lifted from my shoulders.

Thanks, Sam!

IF YOU HAVE ENJOYED THIS BOOK...

Local Legend is committed to publishing the very best spiritual writing, both fiction and non-fiction. You might also enjoy:

GHOSTS OF THE NHS
Glynis Amy Allen (ISBN 978-1-910027-34-9)

It is rare to find an account of interaction with the spirit world that is so wonderfully down-to-earth! The author simply gives us one extraordinary true story after another, as entertaining as they are evidential. Glynis, an hereditary medium, worked for more than three decades as a senior hospital nurse in the National Health Service, mostly in A&E wards. Almost on a daily basis, she would see patients' souls leave their bodies escorted by spirit relatives or find herself working alongside spirit doctors – not to mention the Grey Lady, a frequent ethereal visitor! A unique contribution to our understanding of life, this book was an immediate bestseller.
Winner of the Silver Medal in the national
Wishing Shelf Book Awards.
"What a fascinating read. The author has a way of putting across a story that is compelling and honest… highly recommended!"

5P1R1T R3V3L4T10N5

Nigel Peace (ISBN 978-1-907203-14-5)

With descriptions of more than a hundred proven prophetic dreams and many more everyday synchronicities, the author shows us that, without doubt, we can know the future and that everyone can receive genuine spiritual guidance for our lives' challenges. World-renowned biologist Dr Rupert Sheldrake has endorsed this book as "…vivid and fascinating… pioneering research…"

Runner-up in the national *People's Book Prize* awards.

THE QUIRKY MEDIUM

Alison Wynne-Ryder (ISBN 978-1-907203-47-3)

Alison is the co-host of the TV show *Rescue Mediums*, in which she puts herself in real danger to free homes of lost and often malicious spirits. Yet she is a most reluctant medium, afraid of ghosts! This is her amazing and often very funny autobiography, taking us 'back stage' of the television production as well as describing how she came to discover the psychic gifts that have brought her an international following.

Winner of the Silver Medal in the national
Wishing Shelf Book Awards.
"Almost impossible to put down."

Alison's follow-up book is **DISCOVER THE ANGELS**. In her inimitable friendly style, she gives us many fascinating and heartwarming stories of angelic healing and support for those in trouble, as well as a comprehensive guide to the hierarchy of angels and how we can communicate with them.

THE SOUL CAVE
Sandra Francis (ISBN 978-1-910027-57-8)

Every one of us, Sandra believes, has far greater ability and energy than we realise and in everyday life we only use a small part of our extraordinary minds. We each have the power to create the happy, fulfilled and peaceful lives our souls crave and deserve. Yes, life has many challenges, but we can rise above them and turn them to our advantage, healing the pain of past events and forming new, better relationships. And it's never too late…

Sandra is proof of this. Despite illness and trauma, in middle age she set out on a spiritual path of loving acceptance, forgiveness and gratitude that completely changed her life. In this beautifully written book, she shows us all the way.

LOVE, DEATH AND BEYOND
Helen Ellwood (ISBN 978-1-910027-51-6)

Helen had always been almost afraid of living, believing that mere dark oblivion awaited her in the end. Trained in medical sciences and having rejected religious beliefs, she often felt terrified. But Beryl the hamster changed everything when her soul rose from her body at death, and Helen was shocked into opening herself to the spiritual and the numinous. The paranormal experiences came one after another now and it was soon clear that the human mind was far more powerful, and consciousness far more enduring, than she had imagined. Every reader will identify with the author's doubts and fears, and be inspired by this beautifully written memoir.

Winner of the national *Spiritual Writing Competition*
and Bronze Medal in the *Wishing Shelf Book Awards*
"…compelling… intriguing…" with score 94%.

PAST LIFE HEALING
Judy Sharp (ISBN 978-1-910027-52-3)

Do we live many lives – and could trauma of the past still be affecting our health and wellbeing here and now? The author was completely healed of her own severe claustrophobia in one session and now has decades of professional experience helping others with issues from fear of flying to stubborn weight gain. This truly eye-opening book gives many evidential case studies here, alongside a wealth of information about the concept of past lives across history and different cultures, as well as details of the extensive research carried out in this field.

Winner of the national *Spiritual Writing Competition*.
"A fascinating insight... highly recommended!"
Wishing Shelf Book Awards

HAUNTED BY PAST LIVES
Sarah Truman (ISBN 978-1-910027-13-4)

When Sarah's partner told her that she had murdered him, she took little notice. After all, dreams don't mean anything, do they? But Tom's recurring and vividly detailed dreams demanded to be investigated and so the pair embarked upon thorough and professional historical research, uncovering previously unknown facts that seemed to lead to only one simple conclusion: past lives are true! Yet even that was not the end of their story, for they had unwittingly lifted the lid on some dramatic supernatural phenomena...

THE HOUSE OF BEING
Peter Walker (ISBN 978-1-910027-26-4)

Acutely observed verse by a master of his craft, showing us the mind, the body and the soul of what it is to be human in this glorious natural world. A linguist and a priest, the author takes us deep beneath the surface of life and writes with sensitivity, compassion and, often, with searing wit and self-deprecation. This is a collection the reader will return to again and again.

Winner of the national *Spiritual Writing Competition*.

TAP ONCE FOR YES
Jacquie Parton (ISBN 978-1-907203-62-6)

This extraordinary book offers powerful evidence of human survival after death. When Jacquie's son Andrew suddenly committed suicide, she was devastated. But she was determined to find out whether his spirit lived on, and began to receive incredible yet undeniable messages from him on her mobile phone… Several others also then described deliberate attempts at spirit contact. This is a story of astonishing love and courage, as Jacquie fought her own grief and others' doubts in order to prove to the world that her son still lives.

"A compelling read." The national *Wishing Shelf Book Awards*.

ODD DAYS OF HEAVEN
Sandra Bray (ISBN 978-1-910027-17-2)

If you feel that you've lost the joy in your life and are not sure where you're going, this book is written for you. Sandra knows those feelings all too well. Rocked by mid-life events, she refused to be a victim of circumstances and instead resolved to treat them as opportunities for change and growth. She looked for a spiritual 'guide book' to offer her new thoughts and activities for each day, but couldn't find one – so she wrote it! In this book, and her sequel *Even More Days of Heaven*, we find almost four hundred brilliantly researched suggestions, sure to life our spirits.

Runner-up in the national *Spiritual Writing Competition*.

Local Legend titles are available as paperbacks and eBooks.
Further details and extracts of these and many more
beautiful books for the Mind, Body and Spirit
may be seen at

https://local-legend.co.uk